REDEFINING NEUTRALITY

THE HIDDEN CONNECTION BETWEEN NEUTRALITY AND INJUSTICE

Tomy G Poovattil

Redefining Neutrality

The Hidden Connection Between Neutrality and Injustice

Edition Notice
First Printing

ISBN: 978-93-340-6606-7

Publisher: Self-Publishing

Author: Tomy G Poovattil

Email: thoma6213@gmail.com

About the Author

Meet Mr. Tomy G Poovattil, the insightful author behind the thought-provoking book "Redefining Neutrality: The Hidden connection between Neutrality and Injustice". Hailing from Kerala, India, his journey is marked by diverse experiences and expertise. As an agricultural graduate, he began his professional career serving as an Agricultural Officer in the State Agricultural Department. His unwavering dedication and exceptional acumen propelled him through various positions in a public sector bank, culminating in his tenure as Vice President at a leading pharmaceutical company.

Upon retirement, he redirected his energy towards linguistic pursuits, emerging as a prolific content creator and translator serving government organizations, institutions, and publications. His mastery of English, Tamil, and Malayalam languages is commendable, reflecting his dedication to linguistic excellence cultivated from his school days to the present. For instance, he seamlessly translated complex technical documents, bridging communication gaps across diverse linguistic communities.

A voracious reader and articulate speaker, he remains deeply engaged with national and international events, consistently updating his understanding through regular observation and interaction with a wide range of media sources, including scholarly journals, news outlets, and social media platforms. From this rich tapestry of experience and insight, this book emerges as his maiden literary endeavour.

In his debut book, he delves into the depths of societal dynamics, challenging conventional notions of neutrality with a blend of extensive knowledge and keen observation. Through meticulous examination, he illuminates the complexities inherent in maintaining a neutral stance, particularly in contexts of social and political upheaval. By dissecting historical events and contemporary issues, he unveils how neutrality, often perceived as a virtue, can inadvertently serve as a tool for oppression.

Drawing on his wealth of experiences and expertise, he underscores the imperative of active engagement in shaping a more just and equitable world. He articulates how a passive adherence to neutrality can inadvertently perpetuate systemic injustices, allowing oppressors to manipulate public opinion and sway the majority towards their agenda. Through compelling narratives and incisive analysis, he urges readers to re-evaluate their understanding of neutrality and its implications in various spheres of life.

The author's choice to explore this topic stems from a profound commitment to social justice cultivated over a lifetime of diverse experiences. His journey has provided him with a multifaceted perspective on the complexities of human interaction and societal structures. Witnessing the consequences of apathy and indifference first-hand, he is driven to shed light on the dangers of maintaining a neutral mindset in the face of injustice.

This book serves as more than just a literary exploration; it is a call to action, inviting readers to embark on a journey of introspection and enlightenment. By engaging with the complexities of neutrality in today's rapidly changing world, he challenges readers to confront their own biases and assumptions, empowering them to become active agents of positive change. With clarity, passion, and a profound sense of purpose, he inspires readers to transcend the limitations of neutrality and embrace a more compassionate and inclusive approach to societal transformation.

Contents

Understanding Neutral Mindset
Balancing perspectives and actions among individuals

Traversing Ideological Terrains
Challenges and Strategies

Impact of Neutrality
Exploring the Impact of Neutrality on Individuals and Society

Exploring the Multifaceted Impacts of Neutrality
From democracy to interpersonal and gender dynamics, education and workplace culture

Neutrality Across Spheres
Politics, Business, and Social Justice

Ethical Dilemmas and Challenges of Neutrality

From exploring its implications to addressing the consequences of inaction and reshaping the neutrality paradigm

Introduction

"The hottest place in Hell is reserved for those who remain neutral in times of great moral conflict."

- Martin Luther King Jr.

In the complex fabric of society, where fairness, equality, and advancement intersect, the seemingly harmless facade of neutrality masks its significant impact. It seems to offer impartiality, a refuge from heated debates and moral dilemmas. However, beneath its appearance of fairness hides a significant reality: neutrality isn't always harmless but can silently support the continuation of social problems.

Imagine a world where injustice unfolds before your eyes. A bully torment a weaker child, a powerful figure exploits the vulnerable, or prejudice dictates the treatment of an entire group. In such moments, a common human instinct emerges: the desire to remain neutral. We may convince ourselves that intervening is not our place, that it's "not our business," or that both sides have their story. However, this façade of harmlessness, often rooted in a sense of self-preservation or discomfort, carries a profound consequence: it emboldens the oppressor and perpetuates the suffering of the victim.

Regrettably, a significant portion of society often defaults to neutrality on significant matters that profoundly impact the community, regardless of geographical location or historical period. This phenomenon is observable on a global scale.

This book seeks to unravel the paradox of neutrality, revealing how its seemingly innocuous facade indirectly bolsters the negative aspects of any given issue. Through careful examination and critical analysis, we will explore the ways in which neutrality, far from fostering progress, frequently obstructs meaningful change and contributes to the persistence of social injustices.

Chapter by chapter, we will delve into the complex dynamics at play when individuals from all walks of life, institutions, the press, media and societies adopt a neutral stance in the face of pressing issues. From matters of systemic racism and economic inequality to environmental destruction and political polarization, we will illuminate how neutrality functions as a subtle force that sustains the status quo and undermines efforts towards positive transformation.

At the heart of our exploration lies the recognition that neutrality, as an active choice, entails turning a blind eye to injustice choosing comfort and convenience over conscience and righteousness and maintaining the illusion of equilibrium in an inherently unequal world. By shining a light on the insidious ways neutrality operates, we aim to empower readers to challenge complacency, embrace their moral agency, and become agents of change in their communities and beyond.

Through compelling narratives, incisive analysis, and thought-provoking insights, this book invites readers to reconsider their relationship with neutrality and recognize the profound implications of their choices. By confronting the hidden realities obscured by the facade of neutrality, we can collectively forge a path towards a more just, equitable, and compassionate society.

Furthermore, the book will argue that true neutrality is an illusion. Silence inherently supports oppression and sides with the oppressor. By refusing to take a stand, we become complicit in the perpetuation of injustice.

This is not a call for reckless intervention in every situation. Instead, it is a call for awareness. It is a call to recognize that neutrality, in the face of clear wrongdoing, is not a neutral act. It is a choice with significant consequences, a choice that often perpetuates the cycle of oppression and leaves the victim standing alone.

Join me on this journey as we uncover the hidden consequences of neutrality and illuminate the transformative power of taking a stand. Together, let us embark on a quest to confront injustice, challenge complacency, and build a world where silence is no longer synonymous with complicity.

Understanding Neutral Mindset

Balancing perspectives and actions among individuals

1

What is Neutrality?

"Neutrality helps the oppressor, never the victim. Silence encourages the tormentor, never the tormented"

- Elie Wiesel

Hey there, let's talk about having a neutral mindset. You know, it's all about approaching things without letting biases or preconceptions cloud your judgment. Neutrality in thinking and decision-making is essential for fostering fairness, open-mindedness, and rationality. Picture it like this: you're looking at a situation with fresh eyes, focusing only on the facts and evidence in front of you.

When you're neutral, you're like a detective, carefully examining information, questioning the validity and reliability of sources and making decisions based on what's real, not what you want to believe. It means stepping back from your emotions and personal stakes to see things clearly. You're all about fairness, keeping an open mind, and thinking logically.

We, as neutral thinkers, normally strive to avoid inconsistencies or double standards in our judgments, ensuring that similar situations are treated similarly. We also respect the diversity of opinions, beliefs, and backgrounds present in a given context, acknowledging that people may have different perspectives shaped by their unique experiences and cultural backgrounds, and they value this diversity in their decision-making process.

If we are neutral, we don't rush to judgment. We take our time, weighing up all the evidence before making a call. And we're cool with changing our minds if new info comes to light. Plus, we're guided by principles like honesty and fairness, always trying to do the right thing. Neutral individuals consider the ethical implications of their decisions and strive to act in a manner consistent with moral standards and values.

The concept of a neutral mindset, often touted as a beacon of impartiality and fairness, warrants closer examination. Now, here's the twist: while on the surface, it may seem like a noble stance, in reality, neutrality frequently tilts the scales in favour of the oppressor, leaving the victim side-lined and unheard. While being neutral sounds great, it can sometimes backfire. Imagine a bully picking on someone and bystanders just watching, claiming they're "neutral." That silence? It only makes things worse for the victim, giving the bully the green light to keep going. This subtle yet profound dynamic encourages the tormentor, never the tormented, perpetuating cycles of injustice and inequality.

At its core, a neutral mindset appears to signify objectivity and rationality, suggesting an approach devoid of bias or partiality, where decisions are made solely on facts and evidence. However, in the complex landscape of power dynamics and systemic injustices, neutrality often acts as a shield for the status quo, preserving existing power structures and privileging the oppressor.

Moreover, neutrality can serve to legitimize oppressive systems and narratives by framing them as neutral or objective truths. This normalization of injustice under the guise of neutrality perpetuates harmful ideologies and undermines efforts towards social change and progress.

To truly understand the implications of a neutral mindset, we must acknowledge its inherent biases and limitations. Neutrality, far from being a neutral force, is shaped by societal norms, power dynamics, and entrenched prejudices. It reflects not only what we say but also what we leave unsaid, what we do but also what we leave undone.

Neutrality can even prop up unfair systems by making them seem normal or objective to us. But here's the truth: neutrality isn't neutral at all. It's influenced by society's rules, power plays, and deep-seated prejudices. Sometimes, what we don't say or do speaks volumes.

In light of this understanding, it becomes imperative for us to critically interrogate the notion of neutrality and its consequences. We must recognize that remaining neutral in the face of oppression is not a morally neutral act—it is a choice with profound implications. By choosing neutrality, we inadvertently side with the oppressor, perpetuating systems of injustice and denying agency to the marginalized and oppressed.

So, we've got to be real about neutrality's flaws. Staying neutral when people are suffering isn't just sitting on the fence—it's taking a side, and it's usually not the right one. Instead, we've got to speak up against injustice and stand with those who need support.

The fallacy of neutrality lies in its complicity with oppression. To have a truly neutral mindset is not to remain passive or indifferent but to actively challenge injustice and advocate for equity and justice. It is to recognize that silence in the face of oppression only serves to amplify the voices of the oppressor. As we strive for a more just and equitable society, let us reject the illusion of neutrality and embrace our responsibility to stand in solidarity with the marginalized and oppressed.

Bottom line? Neutrality isn't about staying quiet—it's about speaking out and fighting for what's fair. Let's ditch the idea that staying neutral is safe and start being allies to those who are marginalized and oppressed.

Let's actively challenge injustices and stand up against discrimination. Neutrality only perpetuates the status quo; true progress comes from actively supporting and advocating for equity and inclusion. It's time to use our voices and actions to create a more just and compassionate world for everyone, where no one is left behind or silenced.

2

Understanding the Neutral Mindset across Cultures and Time

"The only thing necessary for the triumph of evil is for good men to do nothing"

- Edmund Burke

Understanding the prevalence of a neutral mindset across diverse populations and contexts requires us to conduct a nuanced examination of various factors that contribute to this phenomenon. While it's challenging to provide a comprehensive explanation, let's shed light on why a significant portion of the population tends to adopt a neutral stance in different territories and historical periods:

Fear of Consequences

Many individuals fear the potential repercussions of taking a stand on controversial issues. Whether it's fear of social ostracization, loss of employment opportunities, or even physical harm, the desire to avoid negative consequences often leads people to adopt a neutral position to protect themselves.

Complexity of Issues

In today's interconnected world, many social, political, and economic issues are highly complex and multifaceted. Understanding the intricacies of these issues requires significant time, effort, and expertise. As a result, individuals may feel overwhelmed and choose to remain neutral rather than engage in topics they perceive as too complex or contentious.

Too Much Info

Thanks to social media and the internet, we're bombarded with opinions 24/7. It's overwhelming, so some people tune out entirely and stay neutral to save their sanity. Navigating this information overload can be daunting, leading some people to disengage from contentious issues altogether and adopt a neutral stance to avoid information overload.

Pressure to Fit In

Cultural and societal norms play a significant role in shaping individual behaviour and attitudes. In some cultures, there may be a strong emphasis on maintaining harmony and avoiding conflict, which can discourage individuals from taking sides on divisive issues. Similarly, societal pressures to conform to mainstream beliefs and values may discourage people from expressing dissenting opinions.

Feeling Helpless

When it seems like the system's rigged against you, it's easy to feel like nothing you do will make a difference. So, some folks just shrug and stay neutral rather than banging their heads against the wall. This sense of powerlessness can lead to apathy and resignation, with individuals choosing to remain neutral rather than expend energy on futile efforts to challenge the status quo.

Sticking to What You Know

We all like to hear stuff that backs up what we already think, while brushing off anything that doesn't. This makes it hard to see things from another angle, so some folks stick to neutral ground to avoid the hassle. This confirmation bias can reinforce neutral attitudes by discouraging individuals from critically examining alternative perspectives or challenging their assumptions.

Losing Trust

Trust in traditional institutions such as government, media, and corporations has declined significantly in recent years due to perceived corruption, bias, and ineffectiveness. As a result, many individuals may feel disillusioned and sceptical of the information provided by these institutions, leading them to adopt a neutral stance as a form of protest or disengagement.

Us vs. Them

The world's getting pretty black and white these days, which makes it tough to find common ground. So, staying neutral can seem like the easiest way to avoid getting sucked into arguments. In such environments, neutrality may be seen as a pragmatic strategy to avoid being drawn into partisan conflicts or ideological battles.

Feeling Torn

When what you believe clashes with reality, it's a real head-scratcher. When confronted with information or experiences that challenge deeply held beliefs or values, individuals may experience cognitive dissonance, a psychological discomfort that arises from holding conflicting attitudes or beliefs. To alleviate this discomfort, some people may choose to adopt a neutral stance rather than confront the cognitive dissonance head-on.

Down in the Dumps

When everything seems messed up beyond repair, it's easy to throw in the towel. In the face of widespread corruption, injustice, and inequality, many individuals may become cynical and disillusioned with the possibility of meaningful change. This sense of despair can lead to resignation and apathy, with individuals choosing to remain neutral rather than engage in what they perceive as a futile struggle against systemic injustices.

It's crucial to critically evaluate the reasons behind neutrality and consider the ethical and moral implications of remaining passive in the face of injustice and oppression. Ultimately, fostering a more informed, engaged, and empathetic citizenry requires us to encourage individuals to critically examine their own biases, confront uncomfortable truths, and actively participate in efforts to create a more just and equitable society.

While these factors help explain why a majority of the population often adopt a neutral mindset, it's essential for us to recognize that neutrality is not inherently good or bad. In some cases, neutrality may be a strategic choice to navigate complex and contentious issues responsibly. But it's worth taking a hard look at why you're staying on the side-lines. Are you really being responsible, or are you just ducking out when things get tough?

Here's the deal, when you sit back and do nothing while bad stuff goes down, you're basically giving it the green light. By not taking a stand, you're letting the bad guys win. That's not a good look.

So, it's time to face the music: staying neutral isn't neutral at all. It's a choice, and it's got some serious consequences. Turning a blind eye to injustice is like giving it a thumbs-up.

Let's face it, staying neutral isn't sitting on the fence—it's actively allowing bad things to happen. We all have a role to play in making things better, no matter how small our actions may seem. It's time to stop sitting idle and start speaking up for what's right.

In a world where staying neutral feels like the easy way out, it's up to us to make a change. We need to break the cycle of apathy and indifference, to be the voices against injustice and advocates for fairness.

Because at the end of the day, neutrality isn't an option. It's time to pick a side and make a difference. Let's roll up our sleeves and get to work building a world where justice, equality, and compassion reign supreme.

When we choose neutrality in the face of injustice, we inadvertently support the oppressors. Our silence and reluctance to act give them the green light to continue their harmful actions. Neutrality isn't just a passive stance—it's a choice with significant moral implications. In essence, by abstaining from action, we inadvertently become complicit in the triumph of evil. To stand idly by while injustice prevails is to betray our moral conscience and neglect our duty to uphold fairness and justice.

It challenges us to recognize that neutrality is not a neutral act but rather a conscious choice with profound moral implications. To stand idly by while injustice prevails is to betray our moral conscience and forsake our responsibility to uphold principles of fairness, equality, and justice.

Even small acts of resistance can have a big impact, inspiring others to join the fight for justice. Neutrality is not an option when faced with systemic injustices and violations of human rights. To create a more just and equitable society, we must be willing to speak out, take action, and stand up for what is right, even when it's difficult.

Understanding why neutrality prevails across cultures and time provides us with valuable insights into human behaviour. But it also highlights the urgent need for us to challenge complacency and indifference. Let's embrace timeless wisdom and answer the call to become agents of positive change, actively working towards a future where justice, equality, and compassion prevail.

3

Illusion of Neutrality: Unmasking Biases and Challenging the Status Quo

"To be neutral is to side with the status quo, to be complicit in maintaining the existing power structures"

- Unknown

Neutrality often gets hailed as this noble concept, right? It's seen as this beacon of fairness and objectivity, this stance that's supposed to be free from any hint of bias or favouritism. But let's be real here—underneath that shiny surface, there's a whole mess of biases and systemic structures at play. They're the ones keeping inequality alive and well, maintaining the status quo while pretending to be fair and square. So, let's talk about why this idea of neutrality is more of a mirage than a reality.

First off, let's address the fallacy of neutrality. Sure, it sounds great in theory—treating everyone equally, no strings attached. But let's face it, achieving true neutrality? That's like trying to catch a unicorn. Every decision we make, every action we take, it's all influenced by a bunch of stuff—our personal experiences, the norms society throws at us, our cultural backgrounds. So, the idea of being completely neutral? Yeah, it's a pipe dream because we're all carrying around our own biases whether we realize them or not.

Now, let's discuss about how neutrality can sometimes act like a smoke screen. You know, it's that thing where biases hide behind claims of being impartial. Take the legal system, the media, academia—places where you'd expect fairness to rule the roost. But sometimes, neutrality just ends up sweeping systemic injustices under the rug, propping up the same old narratives that keep certain folks on top while others struggle.

And let's not forget how neutrality can be a sneaky way to keep things as they are. Instead of shaking things up and tackling inequality head-on, it's easier to slap on the neutrality label and call it a day. Like in politics, where staying neutral might mean drowning out the voices of the marginalized just to keep the peace. Or in the workplace, where pretending to be neutral might mean turning a blind eye to discrimination happening right under our noses.

Privilege? Oh yeah, that's a big player in this game too. Folks with power love to hide behind claims of neutrality to keep their cushy positions intact. Take someone with fat pockets advocating for tax policies that only benefit the wealthy. They'll wrap it up in this neutral package, ignoring how it hurts folks who aren't rolling in dough. Privilege affords individuals the luxury of detachment, allowing them to overlook the realities faced by those less privileged. See, privilege lets folks stay disconnected from the real struggles others' face.

So, what do we do about all this? Well, first off, we gotta call out the illusion of neutrality for what it is. It's time to stop pretending we can be totally neutral and start acknowledging our biases. Then, we gotta roll up our sleeves and get to work tearing down the barriers that keep certain folks down. That means amplifying the voices that usually get drowned out, breaking down the systems that prop up inequality, and actually doing something to level the playing field.

Alright, now let's dig into some real-life examples where this illusion of neutrality plays out. Like in the media—ever notice how they claim to be neutral but end up pushing certain narratives while ignoring others? Take coverage of social movements, political campaigns, or environmental issues—it's all biased in one way or another, shaping how we see the world and who we think matters.

Let's delve deeper into the illusion of neutrality with some concrete examples and incidents across various spheres of society:

Media Bias and Coverage

Media outlets often claim objectivity and neutrality in their reporting, yet biases can manifest in subtle ways.

Social Movements

During the coverage of social movements like Black Lives Matter, some media sources focussed disproportionately on acts of violence or looting, perpetuating negative stereotypes about marginalized communities. This selective framing serves to maintain existing power dynamics by overshadowing the underlying issues of systemic racism and police brutality.

Political Campaigns

During election seasons, media outlets might exhibit bias by giving more airtime or positive coverage to certain political candidates while marginalizing others. This can influence public opinion and skew the democratic process.

In some countries, the media plays a pivotal role in either uncritically supporting government policies or neglecting crucial issues affecting the general public. In India, the mainstream media is often labelled "Godi media," where "Godi" in Hindi means "lap," suggesting it has aligned itself as a mouthpiece for the ruling party and government, echoing their viewpoints.

Environmental Issues

When reporting on environmental issues like climate change, some media sources may downplay the scientific consensus or give an undue platform to fringe viewpoints, creating a false sense of controversy and hindering meaningful action.

Moreover, biased media coverage on environmental issues can mislead the public about the urgency and severity of climate change impacts. By sensationalizing minor disagreements among scientists or giving disproportionate attention to climate change deniers, certain media outlets may undermine public trust in established scientific findings. This can delay collective efforts to address environmental challenges and implement sustainable solutions.

Immigration Coverage

Media coverage of immigration issues can be biased, with some outlets portraying immigrants in a negative light, focusing solely on instances of crime or illegal immigration while overlooking the contributions and challenges faced by immigrant communities.

Biased media coverage on immigration often perpetuates stereotypes and fosters division by framing immigrants as a burden or threat to society. This selective portrayal not only fails to acknowledge the economic, cultural, and social contributions immigrants make but also overlooks the complexities of immigration policies and the humanitarian aspects of migration.

Gender and Women's Rights

In discussions about gender equality and women's rights, media bias can be evident in the portrayal of women in stereotypical roles or trivializing their achievements, reinforcing societal norms and inhibiting progress towards gender equity.

Furthermore, biased media coverage can also contribute to the perpetuation of harmful gender stereotypes and inequalities by underreporting issues such as gender-based violence or workplace discrimination faced by women. This selective portrayal not only diminishes the severity of these challenges but also hinders efforts to promote gender equity and empower women in society.

Healthcare Reporting

Coverage of healthcare topics may exhibit bias by favouring certain medical treatments or pharmaceutical products over others, influenced by financial interests or advertising revenue rather than scientific evidence or public health priorities.

Furthermore, biased healthcare reporting can lead to public confusion and mistrust in medical information, potentially impacting health outcomes and policy decisions. Such biases may overlook important health disparities or alternative treatments, affecting public access to comprehensive healthcare knowledge. It is crucial for media outlets to prioritize accurate and balanced reporting that reflects diverse medical perspectives and evidence-based practices, ensuring the public receives reliable information to make informed healthcare choices.

Let me quote one real-life example of biased healthcare reporting occurred during the COVID-19 pandemic when certain media outlets disproportionately promoted unproven treatments or preventive measures. For instance, early in the pandemic, there was significant media attention given to the use of hydroxychloroquine as a potential treatment for COVID-19, based on limited evidence and preliminary studies. This resulted in widespread public interest and demand for the drug, despite subsequent studies questioning its effectiveness and safety.

The media coverage of hydroxychloroquine was influenced by various factors, including political endorsements and financial interests, rather than comprehensive scientific evidence and public health priorities. This biased reporting contributed to confusion among the public and healthcare professionals, impacting their ability to make informed decisions about COVID-19 treatment options.

Such instances highlight the importance of media responsibility in healthcare reporting, emphasizing the need for balanced coverage that prioritizes rigorous scientific evidence and public health guidelines over sensationalism or partial viewpoints.

International Conflicts

Media bias can distort perceptions of international conflicts by framing complex geopolitical issues in simplistic terms, perpetuating stereotypes and prejudices that hinder diplomatic efforts and peaceful resolutions.

Moreover, media bias can distort perceptions of international conflicts by simplifying complex geopolitical issues, perpetuating stereotypes and prejudices that hinder diplomatic efforts and peaceful resolutions. Additionally, it can amplify polarizing narratives, exacerbating divisions within societies and fostering distrust among different social groups. This biased coverage may side-line nuanced perspectives and alternative viewpoints crucial for informed decision-making and constructive international dialogue. Understanding and critically assessing media portrayals is essential to fostering informed public opinion that supports inclusive governance and effective international diplomacy.

Economic Inequality

When reporting on economic issues, media bias can manifest in the framing of poverty and wealth disparities, either by overlooking systemic factors that perpetuate inequality or by sensationalizing individual success stories without addressing structural barriers to social mobility.

Moreover, biased media coverage on economic inequality can reinforce stereotypes and misconceptions about poverty and wealth. By focusing solely on individual success stories or failures, without contextualizing systemic factors such as unequal access to education, healthcare, and economic opportunities, the media may inadvertently perpetuate a narrative that overlooks the root causes of economic disparities. This narrow portrayal can obscure the broader social and policy implications of inequality, hindering public understanding and policy discourse aimed at addressing these complex issues effectively. Thus, media outlets play a crucial role in providing comprehensive and balanced coverage that sheds light on both the individual and structural dimensions of economic inequality.

These examples illustrate how media bias can influence public discourse and perpetuate inequalities by shaping narratives and prioritizing certain perspectives over others.

Educational Curriculum

Neutrality in educational curriculum can inadvertently perpetuate biases and uphold dominant narratives. History textbooks, for instance, may present a sanitized version of historical events that downplay the experiences and contributions of marginalized groups. By centring the dominant culture's perspectives, educational materials reinforce the status quo and marginalize alternative narratives.

Corporate Policies

In corporate settings, ostensibly neutral policies and practices can inadvertently reinforce existing power dynamics. For example, a company's hiring practices might emphasize concepts like "cultural fit" or "meritocracy," ostensibly seeking to create a cohesive and high-performing team. However, such practices can inadvertently perpetuate homogeneity within the workforce, excluding individuals from diverse backgrounds. This illusion of neutrality masks the systemic barriers faced by marginalized groups in accessing and advancing within organizations. Terms like "cultural fit" or "meritocracy" can serve as veils for underlying biases and preferences, ultimately hindering efforts toward genuine gender and racial equality in the workplace.

Legal System

Within the legal system, claims of neutrality can mask biases that disproportionately impact marginalized communities.

Policing Practices

Law enforcement agencies may exhibit bias in their policing practices, such as racial profiling or disproportionate targeting of minority communities for surveillance and enforcement activities. This can contribute to disparities in arrest rates and the criminalization of marginalized groups.

Bail and Pretrial Detention

Bias can manifest in decisions regarding bail and pretrial detention, with individuals from marginalized backgrounds facing higher bail amounts or being more likely to be detained before trial compared to their wealthier or white counterparts. This can result in economic and social repercussions, including job loss and family disruption.

Jury Selection

Biases in jury selection processes can impact trial outcomes, as individuals from marginalized communities may be underrepresented or excluded from juries, depriving defendants of a fair and impartial trial by a jury of their peers.

Legal Representation

Access to quality legal representation can be biased based on socioeconomic status, with marginalized communities often lacking the resources to afford competent legal counsel. This can result in unequal outcomes in court proceedings, as defendants without adequate representation may be more likely to receive harsher sentences or wrongful convictions.

Sentencing Disparities

Studies have shown disparities in sentencing based on factors such as race, ethnicity, and socioeconomic status, with coloured individuals from marginalized backgrounds receiving longer sentences or harsher penalties for the same offenses as their white or affluent counterparts. This perpetuates inequalities within the criminal justice system and contributes to mass incarceration rates among marginalized communities.

International Relations

Neutrality in international relations can also serve as a facade for maintaining geopolitical power dynamics. Countries claiming neutrality in conflicts may still engage in actions that benefit one side over the other, either through diplomatic support or economic alliances. This selective neutrality can exacerbate tensions and prolong conflicts, further entrenching existing power imbalances.

Environmental Policies

Even in issues as seemingly impartial as environmental conservation, biases can influence decision-making. For example, policies aimed at protecting natural resources may disproportionately impact indigenous communities whose livelihoods depend on traditional land use practices. The illusion of neutrality in environmental policy can overlook these inequities and prioritize conservation efforts that benefit privileged groups.

In both instances, the façade of neutrality bolsters entrenched power dynamics and sustains disparities. To foster a truly just and equitable society, it's imperative to identify and confront these biases head-on. By scrutinizing our own prejudices and advocating for systemic transformations, we pave the way for a future where fairness and objectivity are foundational principles ingrained across all societal realms.

The guise of neutrality functions as a potent mechanism for preserving prevailing power hierarchies and perpetuating inequities. Its camouflage of biases and reinforcement of the status quo hinder genuine strides towards fairness and objectivity. To effectively combat systemic injustices, we must challenge the myth of neutrality, introspectively address biases, and champion equity and inclusivity across every facet of society. Only then can we actualize a world where fairness transcends illusion and becomes a universal reality.

So, what's the takeaway here? Well, if we wanna build a world that's actually fair and just, we gotta stop hiding behind this illusion of neutrality. We gotta own up to our biases, tear down the systems that prop up inequality, and fight for equity in every aspect of society. Because until we do that, fairness will just be another word for keeping things exactly as they are.

4

Neutrality in Everyday Life

"Neutrality may be the refuge of the weak, but it's seldom the right place to be"

- Kirsten Beyer

Neutrality might sound like a safe bet, right? It's often seen as this middle ground where you're not taking sides, not stirring the pot. But here's the thing—when we lean on neutrality too much, especially in everyday life, we might actually be propping up some pretty harmful stuff without even realizing it.

From education and healthcare to interpersonal relationships, individuals across various walks of life may unknowingly uphold biases and reinforce existing power dynamics. From how we educate to how we take care of each other and even how we navigate relationships, this idea of staying neutral can sometimes do more harm than good. Let's dive into some real-life scenarios and unpack how this plays out.

Education is a prime example. In the realm of education, claims of neutrality can obscure systemic inequalities and reinforce dominant narratives. For example, standardized testing is often heralded as an objective measure of academic achievement. However, these assessments may inadvertently favour students from privileged backgrounds, overlooking factors such as socioeconomic status and access to resources. By upholding the neutrality of standardized testing, educational institutions may perpetuate disparities in academic outcomes and reinforce existing hierarchies.

Furthermore, curriculum design plays a crucial role in shaping students' perspectives and understanding of the world. Yet, textbooks and teaching materials may present a sanitized version of history that overlooks the contributions and experiences of marginalized groups. This neutrality in curriculum design perpetuates harmful stereotypes and erases alternative narratives, reinforcing the status quo.

In addition to standardized testing and curriculum design, neutrality in education extends to classroom dynamics and interactions. Teachers may strive to maintain a neutral demeanour when addressing sensitive topics such as race, gender, or sexuality, fearing controversy or discomfort. However, this neutrality can inadvertently silence marginalized voices and perpetuate harmful stereotypes.

For instance, in conversations surrounding diversity and inclusion, a teacher's reluctance to take a stance on contentious issues may signal to students that these topics are bound to affect the equanimity of the mind and status quo and better be avoided as a subject of discourse. By avoiding discomfort, educators miss opportunities to foster critical thinking and empathy, reinforcing the status quo and perpetuating systemic inequalities.

Furthermore, neutrality in disciplinary actions can disproportionately impact students from marginalized backgrounds. Zero-tolerance policies, often framed as neutral responses to misconduct, may result in harsher punishments for students of colour or those with disabilities. This disparity reflects broader systemic biases within the education system and underscores the need for a more equitable approach to discipline.

Healthcare is another area where neutrality can be a real problem. Sure, doctors might try to treat everyone the same, but unconscious biases can sneak in and affect how they diagnose and treat patients. And don't get me started on how policies in the healthcare system can end up leaving certain folks out in the cold, all in the name of staying neutral.

In healthcare settings, neutrality can manifest in ways that undermine patient care and perpetuate systemic biases. For instance, medical professionals may claim neutrality when treating patients, yet unconscious biases can influence diagnosis and treatment decisions. Studies have shown disparities in healthcare outcomes based on factors such as race, gender, and socioeconomic status, highlighting the impact of implicit biases on patient care.

Moreover, policies and practices within healthcare systems may prioritize efficiency and cost-effectiveness over patient well-being. For example, insurance companies may adopt neutral reimbursement policies that limit access to essential treatments or medications for certain patient populations. This neutrality in policy-making perpetuates inequalities in healthcare access and exacerbates health disparities among marginalized communities.

In healthcare, neutrality can manifest in the form of colour-blindness—an approach that ignores race or ethnicity under the guise of impartiality. However, this neutrality overlooks the role of systemic racism in shaping health outcomes and disparities. For example, studies have shown that Black patients are less likely to receive appropriate pain management compared to their white counterparts, highlighting the impact of racial biases on medical treatment.

Moreover, neutrality in healthcare research can perpetuate disparities in medical knowledge and treatment options. Clinical trials often lack diversity in participant demographics, leading to a limited understanding of how interventions may affect different populations. This neutrality in research design contributes to gaps in healthcare access and outcomes for marginalized communities.

Even in our day-to-day relationships, staying neutral can sometimes do more harm than good. Ever been in a situation where something shady is going down, but nobody wants to rock the boat? That's passive neutrality at its finest, and it just lets bad behaviour slide.

In interpersonal relationships, claims of neutrality can conceal power imbalances and perpetuate harmful norms. For instance, bystanders witnessing acts of discrimination or harassment may choose to remain neutral, fearing confrontation or backlash. This passive neutrality enables harmful behaviours to persist unchecked and undermines efforts to create inclusive and equitable spaces.

Similarly, in situations of conflict or disagreement, individuals may adopt a neutral stance to avoid taking sides. However, this neutrality can inadvertently uphold harmful attitudes or behaviours by failing to challenge oppressive dynamics or hold perpetrators accountable. By prioritizing harmony over justice, individuals may perpetuate harm and contribute to the normalization of oppressive norms.

In interpersonal relationships, neutrality can take the form of bystander apathy—a reluctance to intervene in situations of harm or injustice. For example, witnessing acts of microaggressions or discriminatory behaviour in social settings may evoke discomfort, leading bystanders to remain silent rather than confront the issue. This passive neutrality reinforces harmful norms and allows oppression to persist unchecked.

Furthermore, neutrality in relationships can be weaponized as a form of gaslighting or manipulation. Perpetrators of abuse may downplay their actions by framing them as neutral or benign, minimizing the impact on their victims and shifting blame away from themselves. This manipulation of neutrality undermines victims' experiences and perpetuates cycles of harm.

Throughout history, global events and incidents have highlighted the consequences of neutrality in the face of injustice. For example, during the Holocaust, many countries maintained a stance of neutrality, refusing to intervene or offer refuge to persecuted populations. This neutrality enabled the atrocities of the Holocaust to continue unchecked and underscored the moral imperative of taking a stand against injustice.

Similarly, in contemporary conflicts such as the Syrian civil war, international actors have been criticized for adopting a neutral stance that prioritizes geopolitical interests over human rights. This neutrality has contributed to the protraction of the conflict and the suffering of millions of civilians caught in the crossfire.

In the realm of global events and incidents, neutrality often intersects with geopolitics and power dynamics. For example, in conflicts such as the Israeli-Palestinian conflict, international actors may claim neutrality while providing military or diplomatic support to one side. This selective neutrality perpetuates violence and hinders efforts toward peace and reconciliation.

Similarly, neutrality in humanitarian crises can exacerbate suffering and prolong conflicts. Humanitarian aid organizations may face pressure to remain neutral to ensure access to conflict zones, yet this neutrality can inadvertently legitimize oppressive regimes or overlook human rights abuses. By prioritizing access over accountability, humanitarian actors may inadvertently perpetuate harm and undermine efforts to address root causes of conflict and displacement.

In everyday life, neutrality is far from neutral—it can perpetuate harm, uphold systemic inequalities, and reinforce oppressive norms. Whether in education, healthcare, interpersonal relationships, or global events, individuals must interrogate their own biases and actively challenge neutrality when it enables injustice. By prioritizing equity, empathy, and accountability, we can work towards creating a world where neutrality is not synonymous with complacency, but a catalyst for positive change.

So, what's the takeaway here? Well, when it comes to making the world a better place, staying neutral isn't gonna cut it. We've gotta be willing to speak up, to challenge the status quo, and to stand up for what's right, even when it's uncomfortable. Because in a world where staying neutral means staying silent, it's up to each of us to be the voice of change.

Only by embracing this responsibility can we truly harness the transformative power of neutrality and drive positive and inclusive progress for all.

5

Neutrality Vs. Indifference

*"The opposite of love is not hate, it's indifference.
The opposite of art is not ugliness, it's indifference.
The opposite of faith is not heresy, it's indifference.
And the opposite of life is not death, it's indifference"*

- Elie Wiesel

Neutrality and indifference might seem like they're cut from the same cloth, but they're actually pretty different animals. Neutrality is all about trying to stay objective, you know, not letting personal biases cloud your judgment. It's about weighing the facts and evidence before making a call. Indifference, on the other hand, is more like shrugging our shoulders and saying, "Eh, not my problem." It's about not caring enough to do anything about the stuff that's going on around you.

Neutrality refers to our ability to approach situations or issues without bias or prejudice. It involves maintaining an objective perspective and making judgments based on evidence and facts rather than personal opinions or emotions. Neutrality allows individuals to consider multiple viewpoints and weigh evidence impartially before forming conclusions or taking action.

On the other hand, "indifference" denotes a lack of concern, interest, or sympathy towards something. It implies a disengagement or detachment from issues or events, often accompanied by a failure to recognize their significance or impact. Indifference can manifest as apathy, complacency, or a refusal to acknowledge or address pressing problems or injustices.

While neutrality may involve a deliberate effort to maintain objectivity and fairness, indifference typically arises from a lack of empathy, awareness, or personal investment in the outcome of a situation.

So, how do we keep a balanced perspective without sliding into indifference? Here are some tips:

First off, try to see things from other people's perspectives. That's empathy in action. Empathy is the ability to understand and share the feelings of others. By putting yourself in someone else's shoes, you can get a better understanding of where they're coming from and why they might see things differently.

By cultivating empathy, individuals can develop a deeper appreciation for the experiences and perspectives of others, which can help them avoid falling into a state of indifference. Actively listening to the experiences of others, practicing perspective-taking, and engaging in acts of kindness and compassion can help strengthen empathy.

Next, stay informed. Knowledge is power, right? Knowledge is key to maintaining a balanced perspective. Stay informed about current events, social issues, and global developments by seeking out reliable sources of information and diverse perspectives. Get a variety of viewpoints so you can make up your own mind about things. Engage critically with the information you encounter, question assumptions, and consider the broader context and implications of different viewpoints.

And don't be afraid to talk it out. Engage in conversations with folks who have different opinions than you. It's all about keeping an open mind and being willing to listen to other points of view. Dialogue and conversation are essential tools for bridging divides and fostering understanding. Engage in constructive dialogue with others, even those with whom you may disagree. Approach conversations with an open mind, a willingness to listen, and a commitment to thoughtfully evaluate differing perspectives and your positions accordingly, if required. By engaging in dialogue, you can challenge indifference and foster empathy and understanding.

But don't stop there. Once you've got all the info, it's time to take action. Find causes that you're passionate about and get involved. Whether it's volunteering, speaking out, or just lending a helping hand, every little bit count. Neutrality does not mean passivity. While it's essential to maintain objectivity and impartiality, it's equally important to take action when necessary. Identify causes or issues that align with your values and beliefs and take concrete steps to address them. Whether through volunteering, advocacy, or activism, taking action can help combat indifference and make a positive impact in your community and beyond.

Of course, taking care of yourself is important too. Don't forget to practice self-care, whether that means taking a break when you need it or doing something that brings you joy. Maintaining a balanced perspective requires taking care of your mental, emotional, and physical well-being. Practice self-care by setting boundaries, managing stress, and prioritizing activities that bring you joy and fulfilment. Remember that self-care is not selfish; it's essential for maintaining your capacity to engage with the world empathetically and effectively.

And finally, don't be afraid to re-evaluate your stance from time to time. It's okay to change your mind if you learn something new or have a change of heart.

Periodically reflect on your attitudes, beliefs, and behaviours to ensure that they align with your values and goals. Be open to re-evaluating your perspective in light of new information or experiences. Ask yourself whether your actions are driven by genuine neutrality or by indifference, and take steps to course-correct if necessary.

By cultivating empathy, staying informed, engaging in dialogue, taking action, practicing self-care, and reflecting on our attitudes and behaviours, we can maintain a balanced perspective without succumbing to apathy or disengagement. Strive to approach the world with openness, curiosity, and a commitment to making a positive difference in the lives of others.

Neutrality and indifference represent contrasting attitudes towards the world and its issues. Neutrality involves maintaining objectivity and impartiality, while indifference reflects a lack of concern or engagement.

Elie Wiesel's poignant quote captures the essence of indifference, highlighting its profound impact across various aspects of human experience. He emphasizes that indifference, rather than hatred or opposition, poses the greatest threat to love, art, faith, and life itself. Indifference is not merely the absence of action; it is a passive acceptance of injustice, suffering, and inequality.

Incorporating Elie Wiesel's profound insight highlights the destructive nature of indifference and underscores the importance of actively combating it through empathy, action, and dialogue. By embracing empathy, staying informed, engaging in dialogue, taking action, practicing self-care, and reflecting on our attitudes and behaviours, we can strive to create a more compassionate and just world.

From Neutrality to Indifference

The Slippery Slope

Now, let's talk about why letting neutrality slide into indifference is a slippery slope. For one, it can lead to the normalization of injustice. When we sit back and do nothing, we're basically saying that it's okay for bad stuff to happen.

While neutrality is often perceived as an attempt to maintain objectivity and fairness, it can sometimes evolve into indifference, resulting in significant harm to society. Here's how:

Normalization of Injustice

When individuals adopt a neutral stance towards issues of injustice or inequality, they inadvertently contribute to the normalization of such issues within society. By refraining from taking a stand against oppression or discrimination, neutrality can perpetuate the status quo and reinforce systems of power and privilege. Over time, this normalization can desensitize individuals to the suffering of marginalized communities and foster a culture of indifference towards social injustices.

Lack of Accountability

Neutrality can also lead to a lack of accountability for harmful actions or policies. When individuals or institutions remain neutral in the face of wrongdoing, they fail to hold perpetrators accountable for their actions. This lack of accountability can embolden wrongdoers and enable further harm to occur, ultimately eroding trust in societal institutions and undermining the rule of law.

Silencing Dissent

Neutrality can sometimes be used as a tool to silence dissenting voices and maintain the status quo. When individuals in positions of power or influence refuse to take a stand on contentious issues, they may marginalize or dismiss those who speak out against injustice. This silencing of dissent can suppress important conversations and perspectives, stifling progress towards positive social change.

Perpetuation of Inequality

By failing to actively address systemic inequalities, neutrality can perpetuate cycles of disadvantage and oppression within society. When individuals and institutions prioritize maintaining neutrality over challenging systemic injustices, marginalized groups continue to face barriers to opportunities and resources, further entrenching patterns of inequality and marginalization.

Loss of Moral Compass

Over time, repeated acts of neutrality in the face of injustice can erode individuals' moral compasses and ethical standards. When neutrality becomes the default response to instances of wrongdoing, individuals may become desensitized to moral dilemmas and lose sight of their ethical obligations to uphold justice and fairness. This moral apathy can contribute to a culture of indifference, where individuals prioritize personal comfort and convenience over ethical considerations.

The Harm to Society

Ultimately, the transition from neutrality to indifference can have profound consequences for us:

Erosion of Social Cohesion

Indifference undermines social cohesion by eroding trust, empathy, and solidarity within communities. When individuals prioritize neutrality over standing up for the rights and well-being of others, it weakens the bonds that hold society together and fosters a sense of isolation and disconnection among its members.

Exacerbation of Injustice

Indifference allows injustices to persist and worsen over time. By failing to challenge discriminatory practices, unequal policies, or systemic oppression, neutrality enables the perpetuation of injustice and inequality within society, further marginalizing already vulnerable populations.

Diminished Collective Impact

Indifference diminishes the collective impact of individuals and communities working together for positive change. When large segments of society remain neutral or apathetic towards pressing social issues, it hinders efforts to mobilize resources, build coalitions, and advocate for meaningful reforms, ultimately impeding progress towards a more just and equitable society.

Loss of Human Potential

Indifference stifles the realization of human potential by disregarding the value and dignity of every individual. When society turns a blind eye to the suffering and injustices faced by its members, it squanders the talents, aspirations, and contributions of those who are marginalized or oppressed, depriving society as a whole of the richness and diversity of human experience.

Neutrality might seem harmless, but it can easily snowball into something much more dangerous. While neutrality may initially seem like a benign stance, it can lead to indifference and contribute to significant harm within society. By recognizing the potential consequences of neutrality and actively challenging indifference, individuals and communities can work towards building a more compassionate, equitable, and inclusive society for all.

In conclusion, the journey from neutrality to meaningful action requires a deliberate shift from passive observance to active engagement. It necessitates a willingness to confront uncomfortable truths, challenge ingrained biases, and stand in solidarity against injustice. As we navigate the complexities of neutrality, let us remember that silence is not neutral—it is complicit. By embracing our roles as agents of change, by amplifying marginalized voices, and by advocating for justice and equality, we can collectively dismantle the barriers that perpetuate harm and division. Together, let us forge a future where neutrality is not an excuse for inaction, but a commitment to empathy, integrity, and the relentless pursuit of a better world for generations to come.

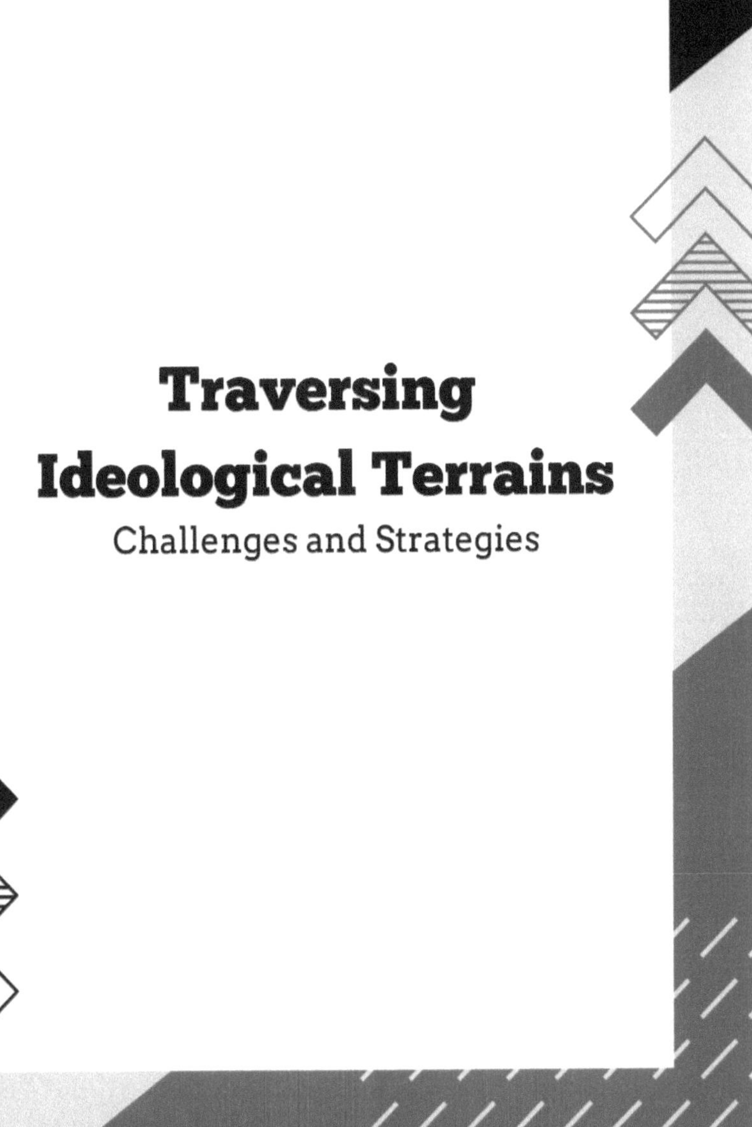

Traversing Ideological Terrains

Challenges and Strategies

6

Navigating Ideological Landscapes: Left, Right, and the Pitfalls of Neutrality

"The world is a dangerous place, not because of those who do evil, but because of those who look on and do nothing"

- Albert Einstein

Left-wing Ideas

Alright, so when people talk about being left-wing, they're basically all about fairness and making sure everyone gets a fair shake. That means they're big on stuff like social equality, justice, and making changes to help out folks who might be struggling.

Left-wing ideologies typically advocate for social equality, justice, and progressive change. We often prioritize collective welfare over individual interests and emphasize the importance of government intervention to address socioeconomic inequalities.

Left-wing policies may include progressive taxation, social welfare programs, universal healthcare, and environmental protection initiatives. These policies aim to mitigate disparities in wealth and opportunity and promote a more equitable distribution of resources within society.

Left-wing thinkers often critique capitalist systems for perpetuating economic inequality and prioritize the rights and well-being of marginalized groups, including workers, minorities, and the disadvantaged.

Basically, they're all about looking out for the little guy and trying to make the world a better place for everyone.

Right-wing Ideas

Now, on the other side of the coin, we've got the right-wingers. These right-wing ideologies tend to emphasize individual freedom, limited government intervention, and traditional values. We prioritize personal responsibility and self-reliance and advocate for free-market capitalism and deregulation.

Right-wing policies may include lower taxes, reduced government spending, privatization of services, and deregulation of industries. These policies aim to promote economic growth, entrepreneurship, and individual prosperity, often at the expense of social welfare programs.

Right-wing thinkers often emphasize the importance of traditional institutions, cultural norms, and national identity, and may advocate for stricter immigration policies, law and order measures, and conservative social values and sticking to old-school social norms.

Neutral Ideas

Alright, now let's talk about the folks who like to hang out in the middle. Neutral or centrist ideas seek to strike a balance between left-wing and right-wing perspectives, often advocating for pragmatic solutions that draw from both ideologies. Neutral thinkers may prioritize compromise, moderation, and evidence-based policymaking.

Our policies may include bipartisan initiatives, technocratic governance, and incremental reforms aimed at addressing societal challenges while avoiding radical changes. These policies aim to bridge ideological divides and promote consensus-building within society.

Neutral thinkers often emphasize the importance of dialogue, cooperation, and open-mindedness, and may critique extremism and polarization on both the left and right ends of the political spectrum.

They're all about finding compromises and practical solutions that work for everyone. So, you might see them pushing for things like teamwork between different political parties, using evidence to make decisions, and making small changes instead of big, dramatic ones. They're big on talking things out and trying to avoid the extreme ends of the political spectrum.

Okay, now here's where it gets interesting: sometimes, trying to stay neutral can actually end up making things lean more towards right-wing ideas. Here's how

While neutrality may initially seem like a stance of impartiality and objectivity, it can sometimes inadvertently lead to the reinforcement of right-wing ideologies. Here's how:

Reluctance to Challenge the Status Quo

Sometimes, a neutral mindset may lead us to refrain from challenging existing power structures or questioning entrenched norms and institutions. This reluctance to disrupt the status quo can perpetuate conservative ideologies that prioritize maintaining the existing social order, even if it perpetuates inequalities.

Emphasis on Personal Responsibility

We might find ourselves disengaging from political activism or advocacy for progressive causes. When we prioritize neutrality over taking a stand on social justice issues, we may inadvertently contribute to the perpetuation of agendas that prioritize limited government intervention and deregulation.

Normalization of Inequality

We might contribute to the normalization of inequality by failing to challenge disparities in wealth, opportunity, and power. When we adopt a neutral stance towards social injustices, we may inadvertently contribute to the perpetuation of right-wing ideologies that prioritize market-driven solutions and individual success over collective welfare.

Failure to Address Structural Inequities

We might overlook the structural inequities and systemic injustices that underpin societal problems. By focusing on consensus-building and incremental reforms rather than challenging the root causes of inequality, neutrality can indirectly reinforce right-wing ideologies that prioritize maintaining the status quo and resisting radical change.

In summary, while neutrality may appear to be a stance of objectivity and moderation, it can indirectly lead to the reinforcement of right-wing ideas by perpetuating the status quo, emphasizing personal responsibility, discouraging political activism, normalizing inequality, and failing to address structural injustices. That's why it's important to recognize the potential consequences of staying neutral and to speak up for what's right, even if it means getting a little out of your comfort zone.

Because at the end of the day, we all play a part in making the world a better place for everyone.

7

Challenges and Obstacles for Individuals Striving for Neutrality

"Remaining neutral in the face of injustice is a silent endorsement of oppression"

- Unknown

Ever noticed how sometimes we just can't help but see things through our own tinted glasses? Our brains are funny things. They've got these quirks called cognitive biases that mess with our perceptions and decision-making.

Ever feel like your brain's playing tricks on you? It's wild how our minds can lead us down all sorts of rabbit holes, right? Take confirmation bias, for example. It's like our brains are saying, "Hey, let's only pay attention to stuff that agrees with what we already think, and ignore everything else!" No wonder staying neutral can be such a struggle when our brains are wired this way.

And emotions? don't even get me started. They're like the secret puppeteers pulling our strings. Emotional attachments to certain beliefs, values, or identities can cloud our judgment and make it difficult for us to remain neutral in contentious situations Ever found yourself so attached to an idea or a group that you can't even see straight anymore? Fear, loyalty, you name it — they all have a knack for clouding our judgment and making it hard to stay neutral, especially when things get heated.

Then there's society, with all its unwritten rules and expectations. Ever felt the pressure to just go with the flow, even when something feels off? Social norms, peer pressure — they're like invisible hands nudging us in certain directions. In environments where neutrality is equated with passivity or indifference, we may feel pressure to conform to societal expectations rather than actively challenge injustices. It's tough to stick to our guns when the whole world seems to be telling us otherwise.

And let's not forget how darn complicated things can get. Social issues? Political debates? Ethical dilemmas? Many social, political, and ethical issues are complex and multifaceted, making it challenging for us to form informed opinions or take decisive action. The nuance and ambiguity surrounding these issues can create uncertainty and indecision, leading us to default to a stance of neutrality rather than engaging with the complexities and implications of the issue at hand. They're like mazes with no clear path. It's easy to throw our hands up and say, "I'll just stay out of it," rather than wade into the mess.

See, when power plays come into the picture, staying neutral isn't so easy. We have less incentive to rock the boat, while we risk even more by raising our voices. It's like a game rigged from the start, making genuine neutrality feel like an impossible dream.

Power imbalances within society can influence our ability to remain neutral, particularly when our interests or privileges are at stake. Those who benefit from existing power structures may be less inclined to challenge injustices or advocate for change, while marginalized groups may face greater risks and consequences for speaking out against oppression. These power dynamics can create barriers to achieving genuine neutrality and foster inequalities within society.

Despite the challenges and obstacles individuals may encounter in striving for neutrality, it's essential to recognize that remaining neutral in the face of injustice is not a morally neutral act.

Sitting on the side-lines while injustice runs rampant isn't just a passive choice. It's like giving it a thumbs-up and saying, "Keep doing your thing." By staying silent, we're basically saying, "Yeah, I'm cool with this." And that's not cool at all.

In many cases, neutrality can be interpreted as a silent endorsement of oppression for several reasons:

Perpetuation of Inequality

By choosing to remain neutral in situations where injustice or oppression is evident, we effectively maintain the status quo and perpetuate existing inequalities. Our inaction allows injustices to continue unchallenged, reinforcing systems of oppression and denying marginalized groups the support and solidarity they need to effect meaningful change.

Complicity through Silence

Silence in the face of injustice can be interpreted as complicity with oppressive systems or behaviours. When we fail to speak out against injustices or actively support efforts to address them, we implicitly signal our acceptance of the status quo and our unwillingness to confront wrongdoing. This silence sends a powerful message that oppression will go unchallenged and unchecked.

Abdication of Responsibility

Neutrality can sometimes be used as a convenient excuse to avoid taking responsibility for addressing societal injustices. We may justify our inaction by claiming that they are merely being impartial or objective, when in reality, our neutrality allows injustices to persist and flourish. This abdication of responsibility enables oppressors to evade accountability and perpetuate harm with impunity.

Normalization of Oppression

Perhaps most significantly, neutrality contributes to the normalization of oppression within society. When we fail to condemn or challenge acts of injustice, we send a message that such behaviour is acceptable or tolerable. This normalization of oppression erodes societal norms and values, making it increasingly difficult to mobilize collective action and effect meaningful change.

In conclusion, while striving for neutrality may present individuals with numerous challenges and obstacles, it's crucial to recognize that remaining neutral in the face of injustice is not a morally neutral stance. Instead, it can be seen as a silent endorsement of oppression, perpetuating inequalities, and complicity through silence, abdicating responsibility, and normalizing oppressive behaviours. By acknowledging the moral implications of neutrality and actively challenging injustice, individuals can play a vital role in promoting social justice, equity, and human rights within society.

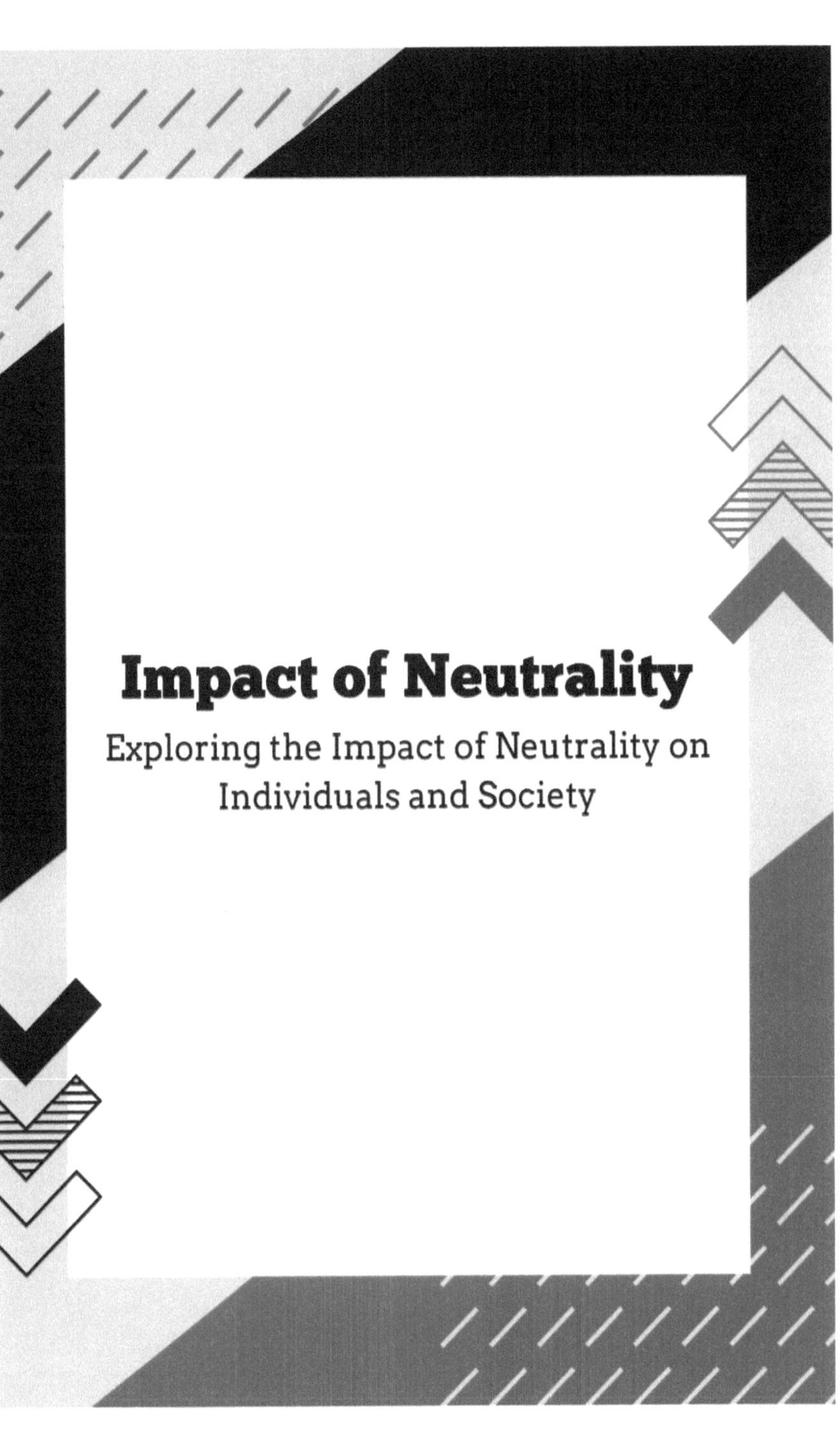

Impact of Neutrality
Exploring the Impact of Neutrality on Individuals and Society

8

How a Neutral Mindset Impacts Decision Making

"In the end, we will remember not the words of our enemies, but the silence of our friends"

- Martin Luther King Jr.

Ever been stuck in that limbo of decision-making where you're torn between different options? It's like being at a crossroads with no clear signpost. You know whatever choice you make will have consequences, and there's no middle ground to hide in. This kind of decision-making dance really drives home the importance of thinking things through and taking action with purpose.

Consider the scenario of a fire breaking out in a nearby house. You've got two choices – either jump in to help put out the flames or turn the other way and hope someone else deals with it. There's no sitting on the fence here; you've got to make a move, and whatever you decide will have a big impact. There is no middle ground or passive option; action must be taken, and the ramifications of that action are substantial.

Now, staying silent or passive in the face of that fire? It's not just standing by; it's like giving the fire a thumbs-up and saying, "Go ahead, keep burning." By not taking action, you're basically saying it's okay for the fire to keep spreading, putting more people and property at risk.

Remaining silent or inactive in the face of the fire carries its own set of consequences. While silence may seem like a neutral stance, it effectively amounts to complicity with the unfolding situation. By failing to take action to address the fire, individuals implicitly endorse its continuation and may inadvertently contribute to its escalation.

Silence, in this context, can be interpreted as tacit approval or endorsement of the fire's presence and growth. Rather than actively working to mitigate the danger and protect those affected, silence allows the fire to rage unchecked, potentially causing further harm and devastation. In essence, by choosing not to act, individuals indirectly contribute to the perpetuation of the problem they are faced with.

Active decision-making, on the other hand, involves taking decisive action to address the situation at hand. Whether it be attempting to extinguish the fire, alerting authorities, or assisting those in danger, active decision-making demonstrates a commitment to confronting challenges and seeking positive outcomes. It acknowledges the role of people have in shaping their environment and the responsibility they bear for the consequences of their actions

Now, let's zoom out a bit. This whole fire scenario? The analogy of the nearby fire extends beyond individual decision-making processes to broader societal contexts. Just as individuals must choose how to respond to the immediate threat of a fire, societies face collective challenges that demand decisive action. Issues such as social injustice, environmental degradation, and political unrest require proactive engagement and meaningful intervention to effect change.

In any decision-making process, the choice between action and inaction carries significant weight. Silence, while seemingly neutral, can have profound implications for the outcomes of a situation. By recognizing the analogy of the nearby fire and the consequences of silence, individuals can better appreciate the importance of active decision-making and the role they play in shaping their surroundings. Ultimately, by choosing to confront challenges head-on rather than remaining passive observers, individuals can contribute to positive change and the betterment of society as a whole.

Analysis Paralysis and Opportunity Cost

A neutral mindset can sometimes lead to analysis paralysis, where individuals become so focused on evaluating every possible outcome that they struggle to make a decision. This indecision can be costly, as it consumes time and resources while delaying progress. For example, imagine a business executive who spends excessive time analysing potential marketing strategies but fails to implement any, missing out on valuable growth opportunities.

Missed Opportunities for Innovation

In highly competitive environments, neutrality can stifle innovation and creativity. When individuals or organizations remain neutral or indifferent towards exploring new ideas or approaches, they risk falling behind their competitors who are actively seeking out innovative solutions. For instance, a company that refuses to embrace emerging technologies due to a neutral stance on change may lose its competitive edge in the market.

Failure to Address Systemic Issues

Neutrality in decision-making can perpetuate systemic issues by maintaining the status quo. For example, in a workplace where there is a culture of neutrality towards diversity and inclusion, systemic biases may go unaddressed, leading to unequal opportunities for employees from marginalized groups. Without proactive measures to challenge the status quo and promote inclusivity, these systemic issues persist, hindering organizational growth and fostering a sense of disillusionment among employees.

Impact on Personal Relationships

A neutral mindset can also impact interpersonal relationships, particularly in situations requiring emotional support or conflict resolution. For example, if a friend is going through a difficult time and requires support, remaining neutral or indifferent may signal a lack of empathy and strain the relationship. Similarly, in conflicts between friends or colleagues, choosing to remain neutral instead of actively mediating or offering assistance can exacerbate tensions and prolong the resolution process.

Ethical Dilemmas and Moral Responsibility

Neutrality in decision-making can pose ethical dilemmas, especially when individuals are faced with situations that require moral judgment and action. For instance, consider a bystander witnessing an act of injustice but choosing to remain neutral and not intervene.

While this bystander may perceive their stance as impartial, their inaction effectively enables the wrongdoing to continue unchecked, raising questions about their moral responsibility and integrity.

Impact on Organizational Culture

In organizational settings, a neutral mindset among leaders and employees can shape the overall culture and values of the company. For example, if leaders adopt a neutral stance on ethical issues or employee well-being, it sends a message that these aspects are not prioritized within the organization. This can erode trust, diminish employee morale, and ultimately hinder organizational success.

In conclusion, while neutrality may sometimes seem like a safe or impartial stance, it can have far-reaching implications for decision-making in various contexts. By understanding the potential consequences of neutrality and actively engaging in thoughtful and decisive action, individuals and organizations can navigate challenges more effectively and contribute to positive outcomes.

9

The Influence of Cultural and Contextual Factors on Neutrality

"Neutrality is not a shield; it's a cloak that disguises complicity"

- Unknown

Let's dive into this whole concept of neutrality and how it's not just some black-and-white thing. Nope, it's all tangled up in cultural norms, societal values, and history — talk about a mixed bag!

Neutrality, as a concept, is deeply influenced by our cultural norms, societal values, and historical contexts. Across different cultures and societies, attitudes towards neutrality vary, shaped by a complex interplay of historical events, power dynamics, and collective experiences. In this exploration, we delve into the cultural and societal factors that influence attitudes towards neutrality, examining their implications and consequences through suitable examples and connected incidents or events.

So, first off, let's talk about cultural norms. Cultural norms play a significant role in shaping attitudes towards neutrality, dictating acceptable behaviours and social expectations. You know how every culture has its own set of unwritten rules and expectations? Well, these norms can totally shape how we see neutrality.

Take some East Asian societies, for example. In our cultures, neutrality may be valued as a means of preserving harmony and avoiding conflict. For example, in many East Asian societies influenced by Confucian principles, maintaining interpersonal harmony (known as "wa" in Japanese culture) is highly esteemed, and individuals may prioritize neutrality to uphold this ideal.

We're all about keeping the peace and avoiding conflict. So, being neutral might be seen as a way to keep things chill and maintain harmony. But flip the script to some Western cultures, and you'll find neutrality isn't always seen in such a rosy light. Especially in places big on social justice, staying neutral when there's injustice going down can be seen as a cop-out, like you're turning a blind eye to the problem.

In Western cultures that emphasize individual agency and social justice, remaining neutral in the face of injustice may be seen as complicity or moral cowardice. For instance, during the civil rights movement in the United States, we criticized those who remained neutral for perpetuating systemic racism and inequality.

Our societal values, shaped by historical experiences and collective narratives, also influence our attitudes towards neutrality. In societies marked by social hierarchies and power differentials, neutrality may serve to maintain the status quo and reinforce existing power dynamics. For example, in feudal societies where obedience to authority was paramount, neutrality was often equated with loyalty to the ruling elite.

Conversely, in societies with a tradition of democratic governance and egalitarian ideals, neutrality may be viewed with suspicion, seen as a barrier to progress and social change. For instance, in the context of gender equality, neutrality may perpetuate gender stereotypes and hinder efforts to challenge patriarchal norms. In Scandinavian countries known for their commitment to gender equality, policies promoting gender-neutral language and practices have been implemented to challenge traditional gender roles.

Historical events and legacies also shape attitudes towards neutrality, as societies grapple with collective memories of past injustices and conflicts. For example, in countries with a history of colonization or oppression, neutrality may be viewed through the lens of national identity and resistance. During World War II, countries like Sweden and Switzerland declared neutrality to avoid being drawn into the conflict, but their actions were met with controversy and criticism, particularly in light of their dealings with Nazi Germany.

Similarly, in our post-colonial societies, attitudes towards neutrality may be shaped by struggles for independence and self-determination. For instance, in the context of international diplomacy, former colonies may adopt a stance of non-alignment or neutrality to assert their sovereignty and independence from colonial powers. However, this neutrality can also be fraught with complexities and contradictions, as countries navigate competing interests and geopolitical pressures.

Now, let's connect the dots with some real-world examples:

The Cold War and Non-Aligned Movement

During the Cold War, many countries in Asia, Africa, and Latin America adopted a policy of non-alignment, seeking to maintain neutrality and independence amidst the superpower rivalry between the United States and the Soviet Union. The Non-Aligned Movement, founded in

1961, aimed to promote solidarity among non-aligned nations and resist external interference in their internal affairs.

The Rwandan Genocide and International Neutrality: During the Rwandan genocide in 1994, the international community faced criticism for its perceived neutrality and inaction in the face of mass atrocities. Despite mounting evidence of genocide, many countries refrained from intervening, citing concerns about violating national sovereignty or exacerbating the conflict. This perceived neutrality contributed to the failure to prevent or mitigate the genocide, highlighting the consequences of indifference in the face of mass violence.

Neutrality in Mediation and Conflict Resolution

In conflict resolution processes, neutrality is often considered essential for mediators and negotiators to facilitate dialogue and reach mutually acceptable agreements. However, maintaining neutrality can be challenging in contexts marked by deep-seated grievances and power imbalances. For example, mediators in the Israeli-Palestinian conflict face scrutiny over their perceived neutrality and impartiality, as historical narratives and asymmetries of power complicate efforts to broker peace.

Neutrality in Humanitarian Aid

In the realm of humanitarian aid, neutrality is often considered a guiding principle for organizations providing assistance in conflict zones or natural disasters. The International Committee of the Red Cross (ICRC), for example, emphasizes neutrality to gain access to populations in need and deliver aid impartially. However, the application of neutrality can be contentious, particularly in conflicts where humanitarian assistance may inadvertently support one party over another. The Syrian civil war exemplifies this dilemma, with humanitarian organizations facing accusations of unintentionally aiding the Assad regime or rebel factions through their operations.

Cultural Relativism and Neutrality

Cultural relativism, the idea that cultural practices and beliefs should be understood within their cultural context rather than judged by external standards, can intersect with attitudes towards neutrality. In societies where cultural relativism is valued, neutrality may be embraced as a means of respecting diverse perspectives and avoiding ethnocentrism. However, cultural relativism can also be used to justify inaction or indifference in the face of human rights abuses or oppressive practices. For example, arguments for cultural neutrality have been invoked to justify practices such as female genital mutilation or child marriage, perpetuating harm under the guise of cultural tolerance.

Neutrality in Political Discourse

In our democratic societies, neutrality in political discourse is often framed as a sign of objectivity and impartiality. Journalists, for instance, strive to maintain neutrality in their reporting to provide balanced coverage of political events and issues. However, the pursuit of neutrality can sometimes lead to false equivalences or normalization of extremist views. In the era of "fake news" and disinformation, the quest for neutrality in media coverage can inadvertently amplify divisive narratives and undermine public trust in objective reporting.

Neutrality and Social Movements

Within social movements and activism, attitudes towards neutrality can vary depending on strategic considerations and ideological perspectives. Some activists advocate for a strict adherence to non-violence and neutrality to appeal to a broader audience and garner public support for their cause. Others argue that neutrality is a luxury that marginalized communities cannot afford, advocating for more confrontational tactics to challenge systemic injustices. The Black Lives Matter movement, for instance, has sparked debates over the efficacy of neutrality versus direct action in combating racial inequality and police violence.

Neutrality in Technology and Ethics

With the rise of technology and artificial intelligence, questions of neutrality and bias have become increasingly salient. Algorithms used in various applications, from facial recognition to predictive policing, are often touted as neutral and objective. However, these algorithms can perpetuate biases and reinforce existing inequalities, particularly when trained on data that reflects societal prejudices. Debates over algorithmic neutrality highlight the ethical complexities of technology and the need for greater transparency and accountability in algorithm design and deployment.

Cultural norms, societal values, and historical contexts shape attitudes towards neutrality in diverse ways, influencing perceptions of its merits and consequences across different domains of human interaction. By critically examining these influences and interrogating the underlying assumptions, we can develop a more nuanced understanding of neutrality and its implications for justice, ethics, and social change. Whether we view it as a moral imperative or a form of complicity, neutrality reflects broader dynamics of power, privilege, and cultural diversity within societies.

So, there you have it – neutrality isn't just about staying out of the fray. It's a tangled web of cultural, societal, and historical influences that shape how we see the world and our place in it. Whether you see it as a moral high ground or a slippery slope, one thing's for sure – neutrality isn't as simple as it seems.

10

The Psychological Impact of Neutrality

"Neutrality may seem like a safe stance, but in reality, it often indirectly supports the negative side of any major issue by allowing injustice to thrive unchallenged"

- Unknown

Let's delve into how maintaining neutrality in tough moral choices and social conflicts can significantly impact your mental well-being. While it might appear as an attempt to stay fair and balanced, it can actually take a toll on your mind and emotions. We'll explore this phenomenon using real-life stories and examples to understand its effects on your actions.

Navigating moral dilemmas and social injustices while remaining neutral brings about profound psychological effects. Individuals grappling with neutrality often experience moral distress, cognitive dissonance, and emotional detachment. Through examining these psychological phenomena and their consequences, we gain insight into the complex interplay between personal ethics, societal expectations, and moral decision-making.

And it's essential to recognize that feeling this way isn't easy, and it's okay to reach out for help when you need it. Within the corporate world, employees may experience moral distress when confronted with unethical practices or workplace injustices.

Firstly, let's discuss moral distress. Have you ever felt like you know what's right, but you're stuck between a rock and a hard place? That's moral distress for you. It occurs when individuals recognize a moral imperative to act in accordance with their values, yet feel constrained by external circumstances or systemic pressures. This internal conflict can lead to feelings of guilt, shame, and moral injury. For instance, healthcare workers may experience moral distress when faced with tough decisions about who gets treatment during a pandemic. Despite recognizing the need to advocate for their patients' best interests, they may feel powerless to challenge institutional policies or systemic barriers that prevent them from taking action.

During the COVID-19 pandemic, frontline healthcare workers faced moral distress when forced to make triage decisions due to overwhelmed hospitals and limited resources. The scarcity of ventilators and medical supplies forced healthcare professionals to make agonizing choices about who would receive life-saving treatment, highlighting the moral complexities and emotional toll of maintaining neutrality in crises.

In many hospitals, frontline staff had to make heart-breaking decisions about allocating ventilators and ICU beds, knowing that their choices could mean life or death for patients. Despite their training to prioritize patient care and advocate for their well-being, healthcare professionals found themselves constrained by hospital protocols and resource shortages.

For instance, in some regions, healthcare workers had to decide whether to remove ventilator support from one patient to potentially save another who had a better chance of survival. These decisions were agonizing and went against their deeply held beliefs about patient-centered care and the sanctity of life. Many nurses and doctors experienced profound moral distress as they navigated these ethical dilemmas, grappling with feelings of guilt, helplessness, and moral injury.

In Italy, doctors and nurses experienced profound moral distress as they grappled with the ethical dilemma of allocating scarce ventilators and intensive care beds, prompting feelings of guilt and anguish over the perceived injustice of such decisions.

Military personnel may experience moral distress during wartime when faced with orders or actions that conflict with their moral values. For instance, soldiers may grapple with the ethical implications of following orders to engage in civilian casualties or use excessive force against combatants. The My Lai Massacre during the Vietnam War stands as a harrowing example, where American soldiers carried out a massacre of unarmed Vietnamese civilians, leading to profound moral distress among those who witnessed or participated in the atrocities.

Moreover, it's not limited to significant events like wars or pandemics—people working in companies can feel moral distress too. Employees in corporate settings may encounter moral distress when pressured to prioritize profit over ethical considerations. For instance, whistle-blowers who expose corporate fraud or misconduct may face retaliation and ostracism from colleagues and superiors, leading to feelings of isolation and moral conflict. The case of Jeffrey Wigand, a former tobacco industry executive who exposed the harmful effects of smoking and the industry's deceptive practices, highlights the moral distress faced by individuals who choose to speak out against corporate wrongdoing.

So, when discussing moral distress, it's about understanding the toll it can take on your mind and emotions when you're stuck between doing what's right and what's expected of you. And it's essential to recognize that feeling this way isn't easy, and it's okay to reach out for help when you need it. Within the corporate world, employees may experience moral distress when confronted with unethical practices or workplace injustices. In the case of the Volkswagen emissions scandal, engineers and employees involved in the manipulation of emissions tests faced moral distress as they grappled with the conflict between loyalty to their employer and ethical principles, leading to internal turmoil and moral compromise.

Then there's cognitive dissonance. It arises when individuals hold conflicting beliefs, attitudes, or behaviours, leading to psychological discomfort and a need to reconcile these discrepancies. Neutrality can exacerbate cognitive dissonance by forcing individuals to confront the misalignment between their professed values and their actions or inaction. For instance, a journalist committed to impartial reporting may experience cognitive dissonance when covering contentious issues such as political corruption or human rights abuses. Despite striving for neutrality, they may grapple with feelings of hypocrisy or self-doubt as they navigate ethical dilemmas in their reporting.

Let me give a real-life situation. Consider an environmental activist who advocates passionately for sustainable living and reducing carbon footprints. Despite their advocacy, they frequently drive a gas-guzzling SUV because it's convenient for their lifestyle and job requirements. Each time they fill up their SUV with gas, they experience a conflict between their stated beliefs in environmental sustainability and their actions contributing to carbon emissions.

This activist may experience cognitive dissonance as they struggle to reconcile their environmental values with their transportation choices. They might justify their actions by rationalizing that their individual impact is minimal compared to larger polluters, or they may compartmentalize their advocacy work from their personal lifestyle choices to alleviate the discomfort of this inconsistency.

However, over time, this cognitive dissonance may lead to feelings of hypocrisy and inner conflict. The activist may feel torn between their genuine desire to protect the environment and the practical realities of their daily life. Recognizing this dissonance can prompt him to seek alternative transportation options, advocate for more sustainable policies, or engage in self-reflection to align their actions more closely with their environmental values.

In political contexts, individuals may experience cognitive dissonance when confronted with evidence that contradicts their beliefs or party affiliation. During the 2020 U.S. Presidential election, supporters of former President Donald Trump faced cognitive dissonance when confronted with allegations of voter fraud and irregularities. Despite overwhelming evidence to the contrary, some supporters maintained their belief in widespread voter fraud to reconcile their loyalty to the candidate with the outcome of the election, leading to the perpetuation of false narratives and misinformation.

In the realm of environmental activism, individuals may experience cognitive dissonance when their actions contradict their professed values. For instance, an environmental activist who frequently travels by plane for speaking engagements and conferences may experience cognitive dissonance when confronted with the environmental impact of air travel. Despite advocating for climate action and sustainability, their personal behaviour may undermine their credibility and integrity, leading to feelings of hypocrisy and inner conflict.

Employees working for companies engaged in unethical practices may experience cognitive dissonance as they reconcile their personal values with their professional responsibilities. Despite recognizing the moral implications of their actions, they may justify their behaviour or compartmentalize their beliefs to alleviate cognitive dissonance and maintain their job security.

Political leaders who claim neutrality on contentious issues may experience cognitive dissonance when confronted with evidence of systemic injustice or human rights violations. Despite their professed commitment to neutrality, they may struggle to reconcile their political ideologies with the moral imperative to address societal inequalities.

Consumers who purchase products from companies known to engage in unethical practices may experience cognitive dissonance as they reconcile their consumption choices with their moral values. For instance, individuals who buy clothing from fast fashion brands implicated in labour exploitation and environmental degradation may rationalize their behaviour by minimizing the impact of their actions or distancing themselves from the consequences. However, this cognitive dissonance may lead to feelings of guilt or moral discomfort over time.

So, when we talk about cognitive dissonance, it's about understanding that inner struggle between what you know is right and what you end up doing. And it's important to recognize that feeling this way isn't easy, but being aware of it can help you make better choices in the future.

And let's not forget emotional detachment. Ever feel like you're shutting down your feelings to stay sane? Emotional detachment is a coping mechanism characterized by a lack of emotional responsiveness or investment in one's surroundings. Neutrality can foster emotional detachment as individuals' distance themselves from emotionally charged situations or conflicts to maintain a sense of objectivity or self-preservation. For example, humanitarian aid workers operating in conflict zones may adopt a neutral stance to cope with the overwhelming suffering and trauma they encounter. While this emotional detachment may serve as a protective mechanism in the short term, it can also lead to compassion fatigue and burnout over time, as individuals suppress or disconnect from their emotions to cope with the demands of their work.

Aid workers responding to natural disasters or humanitarian crises may experience emotional detachment as they navigate the immense suffering and devastation in affected communities. Despite their desire to help, they may feel overwhelmed by the scale of human suffering and adopt a neutral stance to maintain their emotional well-being and professional effectiveness.

In conflict zones, journalists and war correspondents may adopt a stance of emotional detachment to cope with the trauma and violence they witness. The work of photojournalist James Nachtwey, who has documented conflicts and humanitarian crises worldwide, provides insight into the emotional toll of bearing witness to human suffering. Despite the harrowing nature of his work, Nachtwey maintains a neutral demeanour to capture the raw reality of war and injustice, demonstrating the emotional detachment necessary for effective reporting in conflict zones.

Emotional detachment can be seen in the experiences of healthcare professionals working in intensive care units (ICUs), particularly during the COVID-19 pandemic. For instance, ICU nurses and doctors may need to make quick, critical decisions under pressure while providing care to severely ill patients. This intense environment can lead healthcare professionals to compartmentalize their emotions in order to maintain focus, professionalism, and effectiveness. They might consciously or subconsciously distance themselves emotionally from the distressing circumstances around them to avoid becoming overwhelmed or burned out.

This emotional detachment allows them to continue providing essential care without being paralyzed by the emotional toll of their work. However, over time, this coping mechanism can potentially lead to compassion fatigue—a state of emotional and physical exhaustion caused by prolonged exposure to stressful situations and suffering. Healthcare professionals may find it increasingly difficult to connect with their patients on an emotional level, which can impact both their mental health and the quality of care they provide.

Within the criminal justice system, law enforcement officers and legal professionals may develop emotional detachment as a coping mechanism for dealing with traumatic events and disturbing cases. In the aftermath of mass shootings or acts of terrorism, first responders and investigators may compartmentalize their emotions to maintain focus and professionalism in the face of tragedy. However, this emotional detachment can take a toll on their mental health and well-being, leading to symptoms of post-traumatic stress disorder (PTSD) and psychological distress.

So, when we talk about emotional detachment, it's about understanding how shutting off your emotions can affect your mental health and your ability to connect with others. And it's important to recognize that while it might help in the short term, it's not a healthy way to cope in the long run.

So, staying neutral isn't just about keeping the peace; it's about wrestling with these psychological monsters. Recognizing the intricate psychological effects of neutrality and fostering a culture of ethical reflection and moral courage empower individuals to navigate moral ambiguity with integrity, empathy, and resilience. Individuals navigating moral dilemmas and social injustices must grapple with the conflicting demands of personal ethics, professional obligations, and societal expectations. By recognizing the psychological effects of neutrality and fostering a culture of ethical reflection and moral courage, we can empower individuals to navigate moral ambiguity with integrity, empathy, and resilience. It's a tough journey, but hey, we're all in this together.

11

How Small Populations Ignited Major Revolutions & Freedom Struggles while the majority remained neutral or passive observers

"Neutrality is no longer feasible or desirable where the peace of the world is involved and the freedom of its peoples"

- Franklin D. Roosevelt

I n this chapter, let's dive into the stories of some major revolutions and independence movements, but let's switch up the tone a bit. Instead of a dry history lesson, imagine we're chatting over coffee about how a passionate few can really shake things up.

Throughout history, transformative revolutions and independence struggles have often been catalysed by the actions of a dedicated few, while the majority of the population remained neutral or passive observers. These pivotal moments in history serve as compelling examples of how a committed minority can spark widespread change, even in the face of widespread apathy or indifference.

American Revolution (1775-1783)

The American Revolution, which led to the independence of the thirteen American colonies from British rule, was driven by the actions of a relatively small percentage of the population. While only about one-third of colonists actively supported the revolution, their determination and sacrifice played a crucial role in galvanizing broader support and ultimately securing independence. Leaders such as George Washington, Thomas Jefferson, and Benjamin Franklin rallied support for the cause, mobilizing troops, drafting the Declaration of Independence, and inspiring ordinary citizens to take up arms against British oppression.

Boston Tea Party (1773)

A small group of colonists, primarily members of the Sons of Liberty, orchestrated the Boston Tea Party to protest British taxation without representation. While this event sparked outrage among British authorities and inspired further resistance, many colonists remained indifferent to or sceptical of revolutionary activities.

Battle of Lexington and Concord (1775)

At the outbreak of the Revolutionary War, a small group of colonial militia members engaged British troops at Lexington and Concord. While this skirmish marked the beginning of armed conflict between the colonies and Britain, the majority of colonists remained on the sidelines, unsure of whether to support independence.

French Revolution (1789-1799)

Similarly, the French Revolution, a seismic upheaval that toppled the monarchy and ushered in an era of radical political change in France, was ignited by the actions of a passionate minority. The revolutionaries, inspired by Enlightenment ideals of Liberty, Equality, and Fraternity, spearheaded protests, organized demonstrations, and demanded political reforms. While the revolution initially faced resistance from entrenched interests and conservative forces, the unwavering commitment of the revolutionaries eventually led to the downfall of the monarchy and the establishment of a republic.

Storming of the Bastille (1789)

A relatively small group of Parisians, incensed by economic hardship and political repression, stormed the Bastille prison, sparking the French Revolution. While this event symbolized the overthrow of royal authority, many French citizens in rural areas remained indifferent to revolutionary ideals or actively opposed them.

Reign of Terror (1793-1794)

During the Reign of Terror, a small group of radical Jacobins, led by Maximilien Robespierre, carried out mass executions of perceived enemies of the revolution. While this reign of terror instilled fear and obedience among some segments of the population, many French citizens grew disillusioned with the revolution's excesses and turned against the radical regime.

Indian Independence Movement (20th Century)

In India, the struggle for independence from British colonial rule was propelled by the tireless efforts of a dedicated cadre of leaders and activists. Figures such as Mahatma Gandhi, Jawaharlal Nehru, and Subhas Chandra Bose mobilized millions of Indians through nonviolent civil disobedience, mass protests, and acts of resistance. Despite facing widespread apathy and even opposition from segments of the population, the relentless pursuit of independence by these leaders galvanized popular support and eventually forced the British to grant India its freedom in 1947.

Salt March (1930)

Mahatma Gandhi and a small group of followers embarked on the Salt March to protest British salt taxes and challenge colonial authority. While the march inspired widespread admiration and solidarity among Indians, the majority of the population remained passive observers, hesitant to openly defy British rule.

Quit India Movement (1942)

The Indian National Congress, led by a small group of nationalist leaders, launched the Quit India Movement to demand an end to British rule in India. While the movement galvanized widespread support and participation, many Indians remained neutral or wary of risking their safety and livelihoods by openly opposing British authority.

Civil Rights Movement (1950s-1960s)

In the United States, the Civil Rights Movement, which sought to end racial segregation and discrimination against African Americans, was propelled by the actions of a determined minority. Led by figures such as Martin Luther King Jr., Rosa Parks, and Malcolm X, activists organized boycotts, sit-ins, and marches to demand equal rights and justice. While the movement faced opposition and indifference from many quarters, the moral clarity and courage of its leaders inspired widespread support and ultimately led to landmark legislation such as the Civil Rights Act of 1964 and the Voting Rights Act of 1965.

Anti-Apartheid Movement in South Africa (20th Century)

In South Africa, the struggle against apartheid, a system of institutionalized racial segregation and discrimination, was spearheaded by a dedicated minority of activists and leaders. Figures such as Nelson Mandela, Desmond Tutu, and Steve Biko mobilized resistance against the oppressive regime through acts of civil disobedience, strikes, and international advocacy. Despite facing repression and persecution, the anti-apartheid movement gained momentum, drawing support from within South Africa and around the world. Mandela's eventual release from prison in 1990 and the dismantling of apartheid marked a triumph of the human spirit over tyranny and injustice.

Russian Revolution (1917)

February Revolution (1917)

In Petrograd, workers and soldiers-initiated strikes and protests against food shortages and autocratic rule. While a small group of workers, soldiers, and intellectuals actively participated in these protests, much of the urban population remained neutral or apathetic initially.

October Revolution (1917)

The Bolshevik Party, led by Vladimir Lenin and a small group of dedicated revolutionaries, staged a coup against the provisional government. Despite the Bolsheviks' relatively small numbers, their disciplined organization and strategic planning allowed them to seize power and establish a socialist state.

Civil War (1917-1922)

During the subsequent civil war, Bolshevik forces faced off against a diverse array of anti-Bolshevik groups, including monarchists, liberals, and socialists. While the Bolsheviks were supported by a committed cadre of supporters, many Russians remained neutral or passive, preferring to wait and see how events unfolded.

These examples from history illustrate the transformative power of a committed minority in catalysing major revolutions and independence struggles even in the face of widespread apathy or opposition from the majority of the population. While the majority of the population may initially remain neutral or indifferent, the actions of a dedicated few can inspire, mobilize, and ultimately reshape the course of history. As we reflect on these pivotal moments, we are reminded of the importance of individual agency, moral courage, and collective action in the pursuit of justice, freedom, and equality.

It is essential to recognize that the pace and success of revolutions and freedom struggles could have been significantly expedited, or the burdens lightened, had the majority of the population, who often remained neutral or held passive mindsets, actively joined these movements in the interest of the community.

Throughout history, revolutions and freedom struggles have often been driven by the dedication and sacrifices of a committed few. However, the support and participation of the broader population are crucial for amplifying the impact and accelerating the momentum of these movements.

In many instances, the reluctance or neutrality of the majority has posed significant challenges to the progress of revolutions. While small groups of activists and revolutionaries may initiate and lead these movements, their efforts are often hindered by the lack of widespread support and participation from the broader community.

The lesson? Big changes don't always come from big crowds. Sometimes, it just takes a dedicated few to light the spark. But imagine if more folks had jumped in the ring! The road to freedom might've been a whole lot smoother.

Had the majority of the population overcome their neutrality or passive mindset and actively joined these struggles, they could have provided the critical mass needed to challenge oppressive regimes, confront entrenched power structures, and effect meaningful change more swiftly.

Furthermore, the collective strength and solidarity of a united populace can serve as a powerful force for overcoming adversity and achieving shared goals. By rallying behind the principles of justice, freedom, and equality, communities can leverage their collective power to dismantle oppressive systems and pave the way for a brighter future for all.

Therefore, it is incumbent upon individuals to recognize their role and responsibility in shaping the course of history. By actively engaging in struggles for social justice and liberation, they can contribute to the advancement of their communities and the realization of a more equitable and just society for future generations.

So, as we look back on these moments in history, let's remember that every voice counts. By standing up for what's right and joining together, we can shape a better future for everyone.

Exploring the Multifaceted Impacts of Neutrality

From democracy to interpersonal and gender dynamics, education and workplace culture

12

Undermining Democracy: The Perils of Media Neutralism

"When you are neutral in situations of injustice, you have chosen the side of the oppressor"

- Desmond Tutu

Let's dive into a nuanced discussion about the role of the press and media in our democracies. While we often see the press as the guardians of democracy, there's a lot of nuance to consider.

Let's dive into a discussion about the role of the press and media in our democracies. It's not always as straightforward as it seems. While we often see the press as the guardians of democracy, there's a lot of nuance to consider.

The involvement of the press and media in undermining democratic values under the guise of neutralism is a complex and nuanced issue that warrants detailed examination. While the press and media are often regarded as the guardians or pillars of democracy, their influence can sometimes be manipulated or distorted in ways that compromise the principles of democratic governance.

The role of neutrality in journalism and media coverage has long been a subject of debate. While neutrality is often viewed as a cornerstone of journalistic ethics, its application in practice can sometimes lead to unintended consequences. This discourse delves into the complexities of neutrality in the press and media, examining how it can result in false equivalencies, sensationalism, and the amplification of harmful narratives. Through examples, events, and incidents, we unravel the nuances of neutrality in shaping public discourse and its implications for society.

Selective Reporting and Bias

One of the most common ways in which the press and media can undermine democratic values is through selective reporting and bias. While claiming to uphold neutrality, media outlets may selectively report information that aligns with their own political or ideological agendas, while omitting or downplaying opposing perspectives. This biased reporting distorts public perception, undermines informed decision-making, and erodes trust in democratic institutions.

A news channel, while reporting on a political controversy, consistently frames the issue from a single ideological perspective, ignoring alternative viewpoints and presenting biased analysis that favours one side over the other. This selective reporting can shape public opinion in a way that undermines the democratic principle of diverse and pluralistic discourse.

False Equivalency and Balance Fallacy

One of the pitfalls of neutrality in the press is the tendency to present opposing viewpoints as equally valid, regardless of their merit or factual accuracy. In the pursuit of neutrality, the press and media may fall into the trap of false equivalency, where they treat opposing viewpoints as equally valid or balanced, regardless of their factual accuracy or ethical implications. This balance fallacy can lead to the distortion of truth and the legitimization of fringe or extremist ideologies, undermining democratic norms and values.

In a debate on climate change, a news program invites a climate scientist and a climate change denier to provide "balanced" perspectives on the issue. By treating both viewpoints as equally credible, the media perpetuates the false narrative that there is significant scientific debate about the reality of climate change, thereby misleading the public and hindering informed policy decisions.

Sensationalism

Neutrality can also pave the way for sensationalism in media coverage, as journalists seek to capture attention and boost ratings by emphasizing conflict, controversy, and sensational narratives. This focus on spectacle over substance can distort reality and reinforce stereotypes, ultimately eroding public trust in the media.

Coverage of mass shootings and acts of terrorism often veers into sensationalism, with media outlets sensationalizing perpetrators and glorifying violence. By focusing excessively on the perpetrators' motives and methods, journalists risk glamorizing violence and contributing to a culture of fear and mistrust.

Partisan Agenda and Political Influence

Despite claims of neutrality, media organizations may be influenced by partisan agendas or political interests, leading them to prioritize certain narratives or viewpoints over others. This politicization of the press undermines its role as an impartial watchdog and undermines public trust in the media as a credible source of information.

A newspaper owned by a wealthy political donor consistently publishes articles that align with the donor's political agenda, while suppressing dissenting voices or critical analysis. This manipulation of the media for partisan gain undermines the democratic principle of press freedom and creates a chilling effect on free speech and independent journalism.

Corporate Interests and Commercial Pressures

In the era of corporate media ownership, commercial pressures can often take precedence over journalistic integrity and democratic values. Media outlets driven by profit motives may prioritize sensationalism, entertainment, and clickbait over substantive reporting, leading to the trivialization of important issues and the erosion of public discourse.

A major news network, in pursuit of higher ratings and advertising revenue, sensationalizes news stories and prioritizes celebrity gossip over investigative journalism or in-depth analysis of critical issues. This commercialization of the media undermines its role as a public service and compromises its ability to fulfil its democratic responsibilities.

Manipulation and Propaganda

In some cases, the press and media may be co-opted by authoritarian regimes or special interest groups to disseminate propaganda and misinformation, thereby undermining democratic values and promoting authoritarianism. This manipulation of the media can suppress dissent, silence dissenting voices, and create a climate of fear and censorship.

A government-controlled media outlet spreads false information and propaganda to justify authoritarian policies, suppress political opposition, and manipulate public opinion. This manipulation of the media undermines the principles of freedom of expression and independent journalism, weakening democratic institutions and consolidating authoritarian power.

Amplification of Harmful Narratives

Neutrality in media coverage can inadvertently amplify harmful narratives and perpetuate stereotypes, particularly when reporting on marginalized communities or social issues. By failing to critically examine underlying power dynamics and structural inequalities, journalists risk reinforcing harmful stereotypes and victim-blaming narratives.

Coverage of police brutality incidents involving Black victims often frames the issue as a matter of individual misconduct rather than systemic racism. By focusing on the actions of individual officers or victims' pasts, journalists may overlook the broader context of institutionalized racism and police violence, perpetuating harmful narratives that blame the victims and absolve the system of accountability.

Unmasking Support for Anti-Democratic Ideals

In the contemporary media landscape, the notion of neutrality often stands as a beacon of objectivity and fairness. However, beneath this facade of impartiality, there lurks a troubling trend: the tacit support for anti-democratic ideologies under the guise of neutrality. Many media personalities, while professing to be neutral, or by positioning themselves as advocates of free speech absolutism inadvertently lend credence to hateful rhetoric and falsehoods, thereby undermining the very democratic principles they claim to uphold.

This phenomenon is particularly evident in instances where media figures provide platforms for individuals espousing hatred and spreading blatant lies. Despite their professed commitment to neutrality, these media personalities fail to acknowledge the harmful repercussions of amplifying such voices. By perpetuating a false equivalency between legitimate discourse and inflammatory rhetoric, they contribute to the erosion of democratic values and social cohesion.

One of the most concerning manifestations of this trend is the normalization of hate speech. In the name of free speech, certain media outlets provide airtime to individuals who propagate discriminatory ideologies based on race, religion, gender, or other characteristics. Rather than challenging these views, ostensibly neutral journalists often present them uncritically, thereby legitimizing and amplifying messages of intolerance.

Moreover, the propagation of blatant lies under the guise of neutrality poses a grave threat to the integrity of public discourse. In an era of misinformation and disinformation, the media plays a crucial role in shaping public opinion and fostering informed civic engagement. However, when ostensibly neutral platforms uncritically disseminate falsehoods, they not only undermine their own credibility but also sow confusion and distrust among the public.

It is essential to recognize that neutrality does not equate to moral equivalency. While journalists have a duty to present diverse perspectives, they must also exercise discernment and ethical judgment in distinguishing between legitimate viewpoints and those that pose a threat to democratic principles. By abdicating this responsibility in the name of neutrality, media figures inadvertently become enablers of anti-democratic forces.

On February 14, 2018, a 19-year-old Nikolas Cruz, a disturbed individual, opened fire on students and staff at

Marjory Stoneman Douglas High School in Parkland, Florida, United States, killing 17 people and injuring 17 others. In the United States, lax gun laws allow individuals to possess firearms without requiring a license. Many individuals, who proclaimed themselves as neutral and advocates of free speech absolutism, praised these laws. However, amidst this tragedy, Emma Gonzales, a survivor of the attack, delivered a passionate speech condemning politicians and urging them to take action on gun control legislation.

In her speech, Gonzales poignantly stated, "We certainly do not understand why it should be harder to make plans with friends on weekends than to buy an automatic or semi-automatic weapon. In Florida, to buy a gun you do not need a permit, you do not need a gun license, and once you buy it you do not need to register it. You do not need a permit to carry a concealed rifle or shotgun. You can buy as many guns as you want at one time."

She further highlighted the perspective of a teacher, who expressed, "When adults tell me I have the right to own a gun, all I can hear is my right to own a gun outweighs your student's right to live. All I hear is mine, mine, mine, mine."

Gonzales aptly called out those responsible for enabling Cruz to commit such a heinous act, including individuals who sold him firearms and accessories, as well as those who failed to intervene despite being aware of his dangerous behaviour.

We've seen this play out in tragic events like school shootings. While some media figures defend lax gun laws under the guise of free speech, survivors like Emma Gonzales call out the hypocrisy. They highlight how easy access to firearms can lead to tragedy, and how silence on the issue only perpetuates the problem.

To address the issue of biased reporting and the perpetuation of harmful ideologies, media organizations must adhere to stricter editorial standards and ethical guidelines. They should prioritize accuracy, fairness, and accountability, rather than merely striving for the appearance of neutrality. Journalists have a responsibility to challenge hateful rhetoric and misinformation, regardless of its source, and to refrain from granting undue prominence to individuals or groups that seek to undermine democratic norms.

Moreover, promoting media literacy initiatives is essential for empowering the public to critically evaluate the information they consume. By enhancing media literacy skills, individuals can better navigate the complexities of the media landscape and resist manipulation by those who exploit the guise of neutrality for nefarious purposes.

History has shown that fascist regimes like those of Hitler and Mussolini were able to thrive with the support of so-called neutral individuals and free-speech absolutists. The hate speeches of these dictators were amplified by such individuals and the media they controlled. These issues persist in other parts of world including India.

The phenomenon of ostensibly neutral media figures supporting anti-democratic ideologies poses a significant challenge to democratic societies. By amplifying hate speech and falsehoods under the guise of neutrality, these individuals undermine the fundamental principles of democracy and perpetuate social division. Media organizations, journalists, and the public must confront this issue and reaffirm their commitment to truth, integrity, and democratic values in the media landscape.

The role of neutrality in the press and media is a double-edged sword, capable of fostering objectivity and fairness, yet also susceptible to manipulation and distortion. While the press and media play a crucial role in promoting democratic values and holding power to account, their involvement can also be manipulated or distorted in ways that undermine the very principles they are supposed to uphold. By acknowledging the various ways in which the press and media can undermine democratic values under the guise of neutrality, society can work towards fostering a more informed, transparent, and accountable media environment that safeguards democratic norms and principles.

As journalists navigate the complexities of neutrality, they must remain vigilant against false equivalencies, sensationalism, and the amplification of harmful narratives. By upholding rigorous standards of evidence, contextualizing reporting within broader social and historical contexts, and centring marginalized voices and perspectives, journalists can fulfil their duty to inform the public and hold power to account. Only through critical reflection and ethical practice can the press fulfil its vital role as a watchdog

And it's not just up to the media - we all need to be media savvy. By honing our critical thinking skills, we can navigate the news landscape and resist manipulation.

The bottom line? The press plays a crucial role in our democracy, but it's not immune to corruption and bias. By staying vigilant and holding the media accountable, we can ensure that the truth prevails and democracy thrives.

13

The Impact of a Neutral Mindset on Interpersonal Relationships

"Remaining neutral may seem like a safe choice, but it ultimately serves to uphold oppression"

- Unknown

Let's talk about relationships - those intricate webs of connections that shape our lives. You know, the way we approach these relationships can really make a difference in how they turn out. While staying neutral might seem like playing it safe, it can actually have some pretty big consequences for how we relate to others.

Interpersonal relationships are intricate webs of connections that shape our lives and well-being. The mindset we bring into these relationships significantly influences their dynamics and outcomes. While neutrality might seem like a safe stance, it can have profound implications for how we interact with others, often leading to unintended consequences and strained relationships.

Allow me to outline the negative impacts of neutrality:

Lack of Emotional Engagement

Hey, ever noticed how staying neutral in relationships can really mess things up? It's like when you're talking to someone, but you're not really saying anything, you know?

Picture this: You're in a relationship, but you're both tiptoeing around your real feelings because you're scared of stirring the pot. So instead of being honest and open, you're just keeping things surface-level. And guess what? That emotional wall you've built? It's keeping any real connection from happening.

Take a couple who never really get into the nitty-gritty of how they feel. Sure, they might avoid fights, but at what cost? Their relationship starts feeling more like a sitcom than real life – no depth, no passion, just going through the motions.

But it doesn't have to be that way! Being open about how you feel, even if it's uncomfortable, is what builds those deep, meaningful connections. So, let's drop the neutral act and get real with each other. That's where the magic happens.

Failure to Address Issues

Ever been in a situation where you're just like, 'I'm staying out of this'? Yeah, that's what happens when you're all about that neutral life. But here's the kicker – it might seem like you're keeping the peace, but you're actually letting things go from bad to worse.

Let's say you've got a friend who's always flaking out on plans. Annoying, right? But instead of calling them out, you're like, 'Eh, whatever.' Problem is, that 'whatever' attitude? It's not fixing anything. If anything, it's making things worse.

By not speaking up, you're basically giving the green light for the drama to keep on coming. And before you know it, that friendship? It's hanging by a thread.

But here's the thing: you don't have to be Switzerland in every situation. Sometimes, a little confrontation is exactly what's needed to set things straight. So next time, don't be afraid to speak your mind. Your friendships will thank you for it.

Perpetuation of Injustice

Hey, ever been in a situation where you see something totally messed up going down, but you're like, 'Not my circus, not my monkeys'? Yeah, that's what happens when you're all about that neutral life. But here's the thing — staying quiet when you know something's wrong? It's like giving the green light for more drama.

Let's say you're at work and you notice some serious discrimination going on. Instead of speaking up, you're just like, 'It's not my problem.' But guess what? Your silence? It's basically saying, 'Yeah, keep doing what you're doing.'

And before you know it, that toxic vibe starts seeping into everything, making work a total nightmare. But listen up — you don't have to be a superhero to stand up for what's right. Sometimes, all it takes is a simple, 'Hey, this isn't cool.' So next time you see something sketchy going down, don't be afraid to speak your mind. Your workplace will thank you for it.

Erosion of Trust and Authenticity

Ever feel like you're walking on eggshells, trying not to rock the boat? That's what happens when you're all about that neutral vibe. But here's the thing — when you're not being real, people can smell it from a mile away.

Think about it: you're with your family, but nobody's talking about the stuff that really matters — like money or mental health. It's like there's this big elephant in the room, but everyone's pretending it's not there. And you know what that leads to? A whole lot of mistrust and secrets.

Instead of being open and honest, everyone's just putting on a show. But let me tell you, that act? It's not fooling anyone. In fact, it's making things worse.

So next time you're tempted to keep quiet, remember — honesty is the best policy. It might be tough at first, but in the long run, it's what builds trust and keeps those family bonds strong.

Undermining Personal Growth

Ever been in a situation where you just don't want to rock the boat? Yeah, that's what happens when you're all about that neutral vibe. But here's the thing — playing it safe might seem easier, but it's not doing you any favours.

Think about it: you're in a relationship, but you're not really sharing what's on your mind. Maybe you're scared it'll lead to a fight, or maybe you just don't want to deal with the drama. But guess what? By avoiding those tough conversations, you're missing out on chances to grow — both as a person and as a couple.

Imagine you've got dreams and fears, but you're keeping them all bottled up inside. Pretty soon, that relationship starts feeling like it's stuck in a rut. And let me tell you, nobody wants that.

The lack of openness stifles opportunities for mutual growth and understanding, leading to stagnation and dissatisfaction in the relationship. So next time you're tempted to keep quiet, remember – growth happens when you step out of your comfort zone. It might be scary, but it's worth it in the end.

Contributing to Miscommunication

Ever been in a situation where you're trying to read someone's mind but they're giving you nothing? Yeah, that's what happens when everyone's all about that neutral vibe. But let me tell you, it's a recipe for disaster.

Picture this: you're at work, and your boss is just sitting there, not showing any emotion during team meetings. You're left wondering, 'Does she even care?' And before you know it, you're feeling totally disconnected and frustrated.

Same thing goes for relationships. When nobody's being real about how they feel, it's like you're speaking different languages. One person says one thing, the other hears something totally different. And bam, you've got yourself a full-blown conflict. This lack of clarity can lead to misinterpretations and conflicts, as both parties struggle to discern the underlying intentions or emotions.

So next time you're tempted to play it cool, remember – clarity is key. Speak up, say what you mean, and save yourself a whole lot of headache.

Reinforcing Power Imbalances

Ever been in a relationship where it feels like one person's calling all the shots? Yeah, that's what happens when neutrality takes over. But let me tell you, it's not doing anyone any favours.

Imagine this: you're in a relationship, but it feels more like a one-person show. Your partner's making all the decisions, and your input? Yeah, it's like it doesn't even matter. And instead of speaking up, you're just going with the flow, keeping things 'neutral.' But guess what? By not standing up for yourself, you're just letting that power imbalance grow.

It's not just about romantic relationships, though. Whether it's at work or with friends, staying silent when you see unfairness only makes things worse. It's like giving the green light for more of the same. This reluctance to confront power imbalances allows oppression and exploitation to continue unchecked.

So next time you're tempted to stay quiet, remember – your voice matters. Don't let anyone push you around.

Stand up for yourself, and together, we can tip the scales toward fairness and equality.

Hindering Conflict Resolution

Neutrality can hinder conflict resolution within relationships by preventing open dialogue and negotiation. When individuals avoid taking a stance or asserting their needs, conflicts may remain unresolved or escalate into larger disputes. This avoidance of confrontation perpetuates tension and resentment, rather than fostering constructive resolutions.

Ever found yourself in a situation where avoiding taking sides just made things worse? Think about it: when we shy away from speaking up or standing our ground, we might think we're keeping the peace, but in reality, we're just letting the tension simmer and bubble beneath the surface.

Imagine you and your best friend disagree on something big. Maybe it's politics, maybe it's something personal. If both of you decide to play it safe and stay neutral, guess what? That underlying issue doesn't magically disappear. Instead, it hangs around like a dark cloud, casting a shadow over your friendship and building up resentment over time.

But it's not just about avoiding confrontation. This whole 'neutrality' thing seeps into the very fabric of our relationships. It affects how deeply we connect emotionally, how we handle conflicts, and even who holds the power.

We've got to be real about it: staying neutral might seem like the easy way out, but it's actually a breeding ground for problems. It makes us emotionally distant, stops us from solving issues, and keeps unfairness alive and kicking. Plus, it chips away at the trust that holds relationships together.

Instead of hiding behind neutrality, let's embrace open communication, empathy, and being true to ourselves. That's how we build real, meaningful connections based on respect and understanding. It's not always easy, but it's definitely worth it.

While neutrality may seem like a safe approach to interpersonal relationships, its impact can be far-reaching and detrimental. By fostering emotional detachment, avoiding conflict resolution, perpetuating injustice, and eroding trust, a neutral mindset undermines the foundations of healthy relationships. Instead, individuals should strive for open communication, empathy, and authenticity to cultivate meaningful connections built on mutual respect and understanding.

So yeah, while staying neutral might seem like the easy way out, it's actually a pretty big deal. By being open, honest, and willing to speak up, we can build stronger, more fulfilling relationships based on trust and respect.

By actively engaging with emotions and addressing conflicts constructively, we not only strengthen our personal connections but also contribute positively to the growth of those around us. This approach fosters a culture of accountability and mutual support, nurturing relationships that are resilient and enriching for all involved.

14

Impact of a Neutral Mindset on Student Education

"Neutrality is a passive attitude to the world, a disposition to stand aloof from action or interference, not a principle in itself"

- Bernard Crick

Have you ever thought about how your mindset affects your time at school or college? It's actually a big deal. You might think staying neutral is just sitting back and letting things happen, but it can seriously affect how much you get out of your education.

Think about it: if you're just coasting through, not really getting involved or caring much, you're missing out on so much potential growth and learning. But it's not just about grades – it's about becoming the best version of yourself.

In this chapter, we're gonna dive into what happens when students take that neutral approach. We'll look at stories from all over the place to see just how much of an impact it can have. So, buckle up, because we're about to explore how your mindset can shape your entire educational journey.

Lack of Engagement and Motivation

Ever been in class and felt like you're just there, but not really there? Yeah, that's what happens when you're all about that neutral vibe. But let me tell you, it's not doing you any favours.

Picture this: you're in high school, sitting in class, but your mind's off in la-la land. You're not really getting into the lessons, just going through the motions. And before you know it, you're totally checked out.

And guess what? That 'meh' attitude? It's not just hurting your grades — it's holding you back from reaching your full potential.

A neutral mindset among students can lead to a lack of engagement and motivation in their academic pursuits. When students adopt a passive approach to learning, they may fail to see the relevance or significance of their studies, leading to disinterest and apathy.

So next time you're in class, try to get into it. Ask questions, get involved, and find something that sparks your interest. Trust me, it'll make all the difference.

Apathy Towards Social Issues and Civic Engagement

Ever been in school and felt like you're just kinda floating along, not really caring about what's going on in the world? Yeah, that's what happens when you're all about that neutral vibe. But let me tell you, it's not doing anyone any favours.

Think about it: you're in college, surrounded by all these big issues and movements happening in the world, but you're just like, 'Eh, not my problem.' But here's the thing – when you don't care, nothing changes.

Imagine if everyone took that same 'neutral' stance. Nothing would ever get better. But when we all come together and speak up for what's right, that's when real change happens.

Neutrality in education can contribute to apathy towards social issues and civic engagement among students. When students remain indifferent to current events or societal challenges, they miss out on opportunities for critical thinking, empathy, and active citizenship.

So next time you hear about something going on in the world, don't just shrug it off. Get involved, speak up, and be part of the solution. Trust me, it'll make you feel a whole lot better than just sitting on the side-lines.

Without students' collective efforts to address systemic injustices or advocate for marginalized communities, progress towards a more equitable society is impeded.

Limited Exposure to Diverse Perspectives

Ever thought about how staying neutral might actually be holding you back? It's true! When you're not open to different viewpoints, you're basically putting blinders on your brain.

Imagine you're in college, right? You've got all these opportunities to learn from people with totally different backgrounds and ideas. But instead of diving in and exploring, you're like, 'Nah, I'm good.'

Thing is, when you only stick to what you know, you're missing out on a whole world of knowledge. Plus, you're not really challenging yourself to think critically or have those deep conversations that can really expand your mind.

And in class, if everyone's just playing it safe and not speaking up about controversial stuff, it's like we're all just talking to ourselves. How boring is that?

So next time you're tempted to stay neutral, remember – the world's a big, diverse place. Embrace it, learn from it, and watch how much you grow."

Without exposure to diverse perspectives, students' understanding of complex issues remains narrow, inhibiting their ability to navigate the complexities of the world.

Inaction in the Face of Injustice

Ever seen something messed up going down at school and thought, 'Should I do something?' Yeah, that's what happens when you're all about that neutral vibe. But let me tell you, staying silent isn't making anything better.

Picture this: you're at school, and you see someone getting picked on or treated unfairly. Instead of stepping in or speaking up, you're just like, 'Not my problem.' But guess what? By not doing anything, you're basically saying it's okay for that stuff to keep happening.

And it's not just about bullying – it's about all kinds of unfairness. Maybe it's discrimination, maybe it's inequality in the classroom. Whatever it is, when we all just stand by and do nothing, nothing changes. When students choose to remain passive bystanders rather than advocates for change, systemic issues such as bullying, discrimination, or academic inequality may persist unchecked.

So next time you see something wrong, don't just shrug it off. Speak up, stand up, and be part of making things better. Trust me, you'll feel a whole lot better for it."

Without students' collective efforts to address these issues through peer support initiatives or advocacy campaigns, the cycle of harm continues.

Missed Opportunities for Personal Growth

Friends, picture this: you're cruising through college, sticking to your comfort zone like it's your favourite hoodie. But here's the thing – staying neutral, playing it safe, might mean you're missing out big time.

Think about it. College isn't just about acing exams and getting that degree. It's a whole adventure waiting to happen. But if you're all about playing it safe, you might be passing up chances to grow, to discover new sides of yourself.

Take extracurriculars, for instance. Sure, you might think you're too busy or not interested, but diving into something new – whether it's a debate club, volunteering, or scoring an internship – can totally shake things up. These experiences? They're not just resume boosters. They're chances to learn leadership, resilience, and how to roll with the punches.

So, don't just coast through college with a neutral mindset. Take those risks, step out of that comfort zone, and watch how it transforms you. Trust me, the adventure's worth it.

Impact on Mental Health and Well-being

Let's have a real talk about how being neutral in school can mess with your head. It's more than just acing tests and moving on. When you're indifferent about your studies, it seriously affects your mental game.

Imagine this: you're in class, just going through the motions. You're not engaged – you're just there. But this attitude can hit hard. Stress levels soar, you feel disconnected, and maybe even burnout vibes creep in.

Especially in high-pressure schools where being cool and detached about grades is the norm, it breeds mental health issues like anxiety and depression. And the worst part? Feeling isolated in your struggles.

But listen up – you're not alone. There are support systems and resources to help you navigate this madness. Without access to adequate support, students may suffer in silence, risking their well-being and academic success. Your mental health matters as much as your grades. Let's ditch neutrality and take care of ourselves, okay?

Perpetuation of Passive Learning Patterns

Let's talk about how being neutral in class can put a damper on your learning vibe. It's not just showing up and zoning out. When you're indifferent about what you're learning, it's like hitting the snooze button on your brain.

Picture this: you're in class, the teacher drones on. Instead of diving in, asking questions, or digging deep, you're coasting. That neutral mindset? It doesn't help. You end up skimming the surface, relying on memorization rather than real understanding.

It's not just you – the whole classroom vibe matters. If teachers only lecture without involving students, it's easy to slip into passive learning. Without activities like group projects or hands-on learning, it's hard to get excited.

Learning should be exciting, not boring. Let's shake off neutrality and get pumped about diving into our studies. Trust me, it's way more fun when you're fully engaged.

Limitations in Career Preparedness

Hey there, future superstars! Let's chat about how being all neutral in your education game can kinda throw a wrench in your career plans. Seriously, it's not just about getting that degree – it's about setting yourself up for success down the road.

Check it out: when you're cruising through college with a neutral mindset, you might miss out on some serious career-building stuff. Think internships, networking events, career workshops – the whole shebang. Instead of seizing those opportunities to develop skills, make connections, and explore different career paths, you're just kinda coasting.

And here's the kicker – when graduation day rolls around, you might find yourself scratching your head, wondering where the heck your career's headed. Without getting your hands dirty with real-world experience and building up your professional network, landing that dream job? It might be a bit tougher than you thought.

Without proactive efforts to gain practical experience and build industry connections, you may face challenges in securing employment and advancing their careers.

So, let's shake off that neutrality and get proactive about our careers, yeah? Trust me, putting in the effort now will pay off big time in the long run. Let's hustle!

Let's talk about how cruising through school or college with a neutral mindset can really throw a wrench in your plans – from missing out on personal growth to struggling with mental health and career stuff.

But here's the thing: we don't have to settle for neutral. By flipping the script and embracing curiosity, getting engaged, and taking charge of our learning, we can totally change the game. And it's not just on us — educators and schools play a big role too.

Imagine a classroom where everyone's pumped to dive into discussions, where learning isn't just about textbooks but about real-life stuff too. That's the kind of vibe we're talking about. And when we're all about lifelong learning and looking out for our well-being, there's no limit to what we can achieve.

Through fostering a culture of active participation, lifelong learning, and holistic well-being, students can unlock their full potential and become active agents of positive change in society.

So, let's ditch the neutral and get fired up about making the most of our education. Together, we can totally crush it — academically, personally, and professionally. Let's go change the world!

15

Impact of a Neutral Mindset on Working Community

"In times of injustice, neutrality is not an option; it is a luxury that only the privileged can afford"

- Unknown

Let's dive into something we've all probably experienced at work — our mindset and how it shapes our whole vibe in the office.

You might think being neutral at work is all about being fair and balanced, right? But guess what — it's way more than that. Whether you're all about staying neutral or not, it can seriously affect how you climb that career ladder, how happy you are in your job, and even how you feel day to day.

So, let's unpack this. We're gonna chat about how being neutral at work isn't just about being chill — it can have some big consequences. And trust me, we've got some juicy examples and stories to back it up. So, buckle up and let's get into it!

Stagnation in Career Progression

Let's talk about something that hits close to home for a lot of us – our careers. Ever felt like you're stuck in a rut at work, not moving forward like you'd hoped? Well, it might just be because of that neutral mindset you've been rocking.

Here's the deal: when we're all about staying low-key and not speaking up for ourselves, it can seriously hold us back. Think about it – if you're not putting yourself out there, advocating for what you deserve, how can you expect to move up the ladder?

Especially in big companies, it's all about who you know and how you sell yourself. So, if you're not networking, shouting about your achievements, or pushing for those juicy opportunities, chances are you're gonna be stuck in the same old spot.

But hey, it's not all doom and gloom. By shaking off that neutral vibe and getting proactive about our careers – whether it's finding a mentor, seeking out training, or just shouting our accomplishments from the rooftops – we can totally break free from that stagnation and start climbing that career ladder like a boss. So, let's do this!

Gendered Expectations and Stereotypes

Let's dive into something that's all too real for a lot of working women out there — gender expectations in the workplace. Ever felt like you've gotta tone down your personality just to fit in? Yeah, that's what we're talking about.

Here's the scoop: when women play it neutral at work, trying not to rock the boat or seem too pushy, it can actually backfire big time. Instead of being seen as leaders, they might get labelled as not ambitious enough or lacking that "go-getter" attitude.

Especially in industries where guys seem to rule the roost — like tech or finance — it can feel like an uphill battle. Women who try to navigate the workplace without making waves might find themselves hitting glass ceilings left and right. Even if they've got the skills and smarts for the top jobs, those gender stereotypes can be tough to shake.

But here's the thing — we're not just gonna sit back and let that happen. By owning our strengths, speaking up, and refusing to play by those outdated rules, we can start tearing down those barriers and showing the world what we're made of. So, let's kick those gendered expectations to the curb and start making some real waves!

Undermining Confidence and Self-Efficacy

Alright, let's get real about something that affects way too many folks in the workplace – confidence. Ever felt like you've got something to say but held back because you weren't sure how it'd go down? Yeah, that's what we're diving into.

Here's the deal: when we're all about staying neutral at work, keeping quiet instead of speaking up, it can seriously mess with our heads. We start doubting ourselves, feeling like we're not good enough or like we're just faking it.

Now, imagine you're in a team meeting, and you've got this killer idea brewing. But because you're from a background that's not exactly front and centre, you hesitate. You worry about what folks will think, if they'll take you seriously. So, you keep quiet. And guess what? It eats away your confidence, makes you feel like you don't belong.

But here's the thing – your voice matters. And yeah, speaking up can be scary, especially when you're worried about backlash or being dismissed. But staying silent? That's not an option. So, let's break free from that neutral mindset, own our voices, and show the world what we're made of. You've got this!

Contributing to Organizational Inertia

Let's talk about something that can really hold a company back – playing it neutral in the workplace. Ever felt like things could be done better, but you're not sure if it's worth speaking up? Yeah, that's what we're diving into.

Here's the scoop: when everyone's all about sticking to the same old routine, not pushing for change or speaking up with fresh ideas, it's like hitting the brakes on progress. Companies can get stuck in their ways, missing out on opportunities to grow and adapt to what's happening in the world.

Now, picture this: you're in a company that's all about doing things the way they've always been done. You see a better way, but because you're all about playing it safe, you keep quiet. And what happens? The company falls behind, fails to keep up with the competition.

But here's the thing – staying neutral when it comes to change? It's not gonna cut it. Companies need folks who are willing to shake things up, try out new ideas, and take risks. So let's break free from that neutral mindset, spark some innovation, and help our companies thrive in a fast-changing world. Without a culture of innovation and risk-taking, companies risk falling behind their competitors and stagnating in the marketplace. It's time to shake things up!

Reinforcement of Gender Pay Gap

Let's get down to something that's been a thorn in the side of workplace equality for way too long – the gender pay gap. Ever wondered why women often end up with smaller pay checks and fewer chances to move up the ladder? Well, it's got a lot to do with that whole staying-neutral-at-work thing.

Here's the deal: when we're all about playing it cool instead of pushing for what we're worth, it just reinforces the gap. Especially for women, who might feel like they've gotta stay quiet to avoid rocking the boat. But here's the harsh truth – when we don't speak up about our pay or fight for those promotions, we're basically saying it's okay to keep paying us less.

In various industries, studies have consistently shown that women are less likely than men to negotiate their salaries or pursue promotions, often citing concerns about being perceived as pushy or disruptive. This reluctance to assert their value directly contributes to the gender pay gap, where women earn less than their male counterparts for comparable work.

And it's not just a feeling – studies have shown it too. Women are way less likely than men to speak up about their salaries or go after those top jobs, worried about coming off as too aggressive. But that hesitation? It's a big reason why women still earn less than men for doing the same work.

For instance, the findings of a study conducted by the Institute for Women's Policy Research (IWPR) based in Washington D.C. underscore the significant impact of gender bias on negotiation behaviours and its repercussions on pay equity. They dug into how gender bias plays out in negotiations, and let's just say, the results were eye-opening. So, let's stop staying neutral and start demanding what we deserve. It's time to close that pay gap once and for all!

Let's examine a few of these findings

Let's dive into the tech scene, where the gender pay gap is alive and kicking. Picture this — a female software whiz finds out she's making way less than her male counterparts, even though they're all bringing similar skills to the table. So, she gathers her courage and brings it up with her boss.

But instead of getting support, she gets shut down, made to feel like she's asking for too much. Worried about rocking the boat, she decides to let it slide, adding another notch to that gender pay gap belt. It's a tough reality in

Silicon Valley and beyond, but it's time to call it out and demand change.

Now, let's talk about the finance world, where climbing that career ladder can feel like an uphill battle, especially for women. Take this female investment whiz, for instance. She's killing it, smashing targets left and right, but when it comes to moving up the ranks, she hesitates. Why? Because she's worried about being seen as too ambitious or pushy. Meanwhile, her male colleagues are gunning for those promotions without a second thought. So, she stays put, watching them zoom past her while she's stuck in the same old spot. It's a frustrating cycle that's keeping women from reaching their full potential in finance. But it's time to break free from those old-school stereotypes and demand the recognition we deserve. Let's shake things up!

Let's chat about academia, where the gender gap is alive and kicking. Imagine this — a brilliant female professor gets a job offer from a top-notch university. But when it comes to negotiating her salary, she hesitates. Why? Because she's worried about rocking the boat, about how it'll look to her new colleagues. So, she settles for the first offer, not realizing that her male counterparts are pulling in way more for the same gig. It's a frustrating reality that's keeping women from getting their fair share in academia. But it's time to shake things up and demand equal pay for equal work. Let's break those barriers!

These examples underscore the pervasive nature of gender bias and the reluctance of women to assert their value in various industries, ultimately contributing to the persistence of the gender pay gap.

Exacerbation of Workplace Harassment and Discrimination

Let's discuss about something that's tough to swallow – workplace harassment and discrimination. Picture this: when folks stay neutral in the face of bad behaviour, it just makes things worse. You've got folks brushing off inappropriate comments or turning a blind eye to discrimination, and guess what? It just gives the green light for more of the same.

And here's where it gets even trickier – when nobody speaks up, victims feel like they've got nobody to turn to. They're scared of speaking out, worried about what might happen if they do. So, they stay quiet, and the cycle continues.

But here's the deal – staying neutral when it comes to harassment and discrimination? It's not an option. We've gotta speak up, call out bad behaviour, and support those who've been targeted. It's the only way we're gonna make our workplaces safe and inclusive for everyone. So, let's break that silence and stand up for what's right.

Erosion of Organizational Values and Ethics

Let's get real about something that can really mess with a company's mojo — eroding values and ethics in the workplace. Imagine this: when folks are all about staying neutral, even when they see shady stuff going down, it's like giving the thumbs up to bad behaviour.

Here's the kicker — when we put neutrality above doing what's right, it's like we're selling out our company's integrity. And trust me, that's a slippery slope to a tarnished reputation.

Think about it — when you turn a blind eye to fraud or corruption, it's not just the company that suffers. It's everyone involved, from employees to customers to the community.

So, here's the bottom line — we can't just sit back and let unethical stuff slide. We've gotta speak up, hold ourselves and our co-workers accountable, and make sure our company's values are more than just words on a poster. It's time to take a stand for what's right!

Hindrance to Innovation and Creativity

Let's talk about how being all "meh" at work can seriously put a damper on creativity and innovation. Picture this: you're in a meeting, tossing around ideas, but everyone's playing it safe, sticking to the same old routine. Sound familiar?

Here's the scoop: when we're all about staying neutral, not rocking the boat with new ideas or pushing back against the norm, it's like putting a lid on creativity. We miss out on that spark of innovation that comes from different perspectives and lively debate.

So, next time you're in a brainstorming session, don't hold back. Let those wild ideas fly, challenge the status quo, and see where it takes you. Because let's face it – it's those out-of-the-box ideas that shake things up and lead to real breakthroughs. Let's get creative, folks!

Let's get real about how being neutral at work can seriously mess things up for everyone. It's not just about playing it safe – it's about missing out on real opportunities for change and growth.

Check it out: when we're all about staying neutral, we're basically giving the green light to all sorts of problems – from gender inequality to harassment to just plain old boring ideas. But here's the good news – we don't have to settle for that.

By stepping up and speaking out, we can create workplaces where everyone's voice is heard, where diversity and innovation are celebrated, and where doing the right thing is non-negotiable. It's about building a culture of accountability, fairness, and respect.

Through fostering a culture of inclusivity, transparency, and integrity, companies can cultivate environments where employees can thrive professionally and ethically, while advancing the collective interests of the organization.

So, let's ditch the neutrality and start making some noise. Together, we can create workplaces where everyone can thrive and where our collective success is built on a foundation of inclusivity, transparency, and integrity. Let's do this!

16

The Impact of a Neutral Mindset on Women

"In a world plagued by injustice, neutrality is not an option—it's a privilege that must be relinquished in the pursuit of justice"

- Unknown

The mindset that we adopt in our roles at home and in society can profoundly influence their experiences and opportunities. Being neutral might seem like just sitting on the fence, but it actually has a big effect on how we feel, how we connect with others, and what they can do in society. In this chapter, we're going to dive into what it means when women take on a neutral mindset, pointing out some real-life examples and situations that show why it's important.

Reinforcement of Gender Roles and Expectations

Let's talk about how sticking with a neutral mindset can actually keep old-fashioned gender roles and expectations going strong. When women stay neutral instead of pushing back against unfair norms or fighting for equality, it can end up keeping things just the way they are.

Think about it: in lots of places, women who go along with the traditional roles of taking care of the home and the family might not speak up against the unfair expectations placed on them. By staying neutral, they're basically saying it's okay for things to stay unequal. This means they keep getting stuck with most of the household chores and childcare duties, which stops them from chasing their own dreams, both personally and professionally.

Acceptance of Inequality and Discrimination

Let's talk about how staying neutral can actually make it easier to accept unfairness and discrimination in our lives, whether it's at work or in social situations. When women don't speak up against unfair treatment or fight for what they deserve, it can make them feel like they don't have any power and they just have to put up with it.

In some places where women already face a lot of barriers to things like education, jobs, and being involved in politics, those who stay neutral about gender inequality might just end up accepting their second-class status. But by accepting discrimination, they're just keeping that cycle of unfairness going, and it makes it harder for things to change and for women to have more control over their lives.

Limitation of Leadership and Assertiveness

Let's chat about how keeping a neutral mindset can hold women back from really going after leadership roles and being assertive, which can slow down their career progress and impact. When women hold back from speaking up or standing up for themselves, they can end up missing out on chances to grow in their careers and get the recognition they deserve.

Picture this: in big companies, women who don't push themselves forward or show how capable they are might get overlooked for promotions or fair pay. Without speaking up for themselves and showing that they've got what it takes, they could find it tough to move up the ladder, especially in fields where men call most of the shots.

Perpetuation of Internalized Misogyny

Let's talk about how staying neutral can actually feed into something called internalized misogyny, where women start to believe all the sexist stuff society throws at them. When women don't stand up against unfair rules and fight for equality, they're kind of adding to their own struggles without even realizing it.

Think about it: in places where women are taught to see each other as competition for guys' attention and approval, those who stay neutral about feminist movements might not see the point in fighting against the sexism that holds them back. But by going along with it, they're basically making it harder for all women to come together and make things better for everyone.

Perpetuation of Domestic Labour Disparities

Let's dive into how staying neutral about household chores can actually keep things unequal for women, with them shouldering most of the burden. When women don't push back against old-fashioned ideas about who should do what at home, they end up reinforcing the idea that it's mainly their job to take care of everything.

Imagine this: in homes where women want to keep the peace and avoid arguments, they might not speak up about needing help with chores from their partners. But by staying neutral, they're basically saying it's okay for women to do most of the cooking, cleaning, and looking after the kids, which leaves them with less time and energy for their own goals and career growth.

Impact on Mental Health and Well-being

Let's talk about how staying neutral in certain situations can really take a toll on women's mental health and happiness. When women keep their own needs and feelings quiet to keep the peace or fit into certain roles, it can lead to burnout, stress, and just feeling downright unhappy.

Think about it: in places where women are taught to always put others first and ignore their own wants, those who stay neutral about taking care of themselves might end up feeling stressed out and emotionally drained all the time. Without making their own well-being a priority and asking for help when they need it, they could be silently struggling, which isn't good for their mental health or their overall quality of life.

Hindrance to Collective Action and Advocacy

Let's talk about how staying neutral can actually get in the way of women coming together to fight for equality and justice. When women don't speak up against unfair treatment or join movements for change, they're basically keeping the same old systems of oppression going and making it harder for everyone to stand together and make a difference.

Picture this: in places where women are up against laws and rules that hold them back, those who stay neutral about feminist movements might miss out on chances to push for better policies and make their voices heard. Without coming together and speaking out, progress towards equality gets slowed down, and women keep on facing the same old discrimination and being pushed to the side-lines.

Limited Representation and Visibility

Let's talk about how staying neutral can keep women from being seen and heard in important places like politics, media, and leadership roles. When women don't stand up for themselves and push for their rights, they end up missing out on chances to be part of decision-making and public discussions.

Imagine this: in places where women are told to stay quiet and stay out of politics, those who stay neutral about getting involved might stay on the side-lines, leaving fewer women in positions where they can make a difference. Without different voices and viewpoints in power, the decisions made might not take into account what women really need and want.

The impact of this neutral stance on women is pretty big, from keeping unfair household chores going to making it harder for women to feel good mentally and stopping them from joining together to fight for what's right. But if we all start recognizing the importance of speaking up and supporting each other, we can create a world where women aren't held back, where they can challenge the norms and go after their dreams freely. By making sure everyone's included and treated equally, we can use the power of women coming together to make some real positive changes and make the world fairer for everyone.

It's crucial to dismantle the barriers that prevent women from achieving their full potential. When women are empowered to voice their concerns and unite in solidarity, they can drive meaningful progress towards gender equality and create a more just society where everyone has equal opportunities to thrive. Through collective action and mutual support, we can harness the strength of diversity and inclusivity to build a future where all individuals are valued and respected.

Neutrality Across Spheres

Politics, Business, and Social Justice

17

Neutrality in Politics and Governance

"Neutrality is a passive attitude to the world, a disposition to stand aloof from action or interference, not a principle in itself"

- Bernard Crick

Neutrality in politics and governance is often perceived as a stance of impartiality and objectivity, yet it can paradoxically lead to inaction or complicity in the face of injustice. This discourse delves into the complexities of political neutrality, examining its implications for policy-making, social progress, and the perpetuation of systemic inequalities. Through suitable examples, incidents, and events, we unravel the intricate dynamics of neutrality in shaping political decisions and governance structures.

Neutrality and Inaction in the Face of Injustice

Political neutrality can sometimes manifest as a reluctance to take decisive action in response to social injustices or human rights abuses. In the pursuit of maintaining a semblance of impartiality, politicians and policymakers may choose to remain passive or neutral, thereby perpetuating systemic inequalities and failing to address pressing issues. For example, in the context of police brutality and racial injustice, political leaders who adopt a neutral stance may inadvertently condone or enable the disproportionate use of force against marginalized communities.

In the aftermath of the killing of George Floyd by police officers in Minneapolis, Minnesota, in May 2020, many political leaders initially responded with statements of neutrality or equivocation. Some elected officials refrained from condemning the actions of law enforcement or endorsing calls for police reform, citing a desire to wait for more information or maintain neutrality in the face of ongoing protests. However, this neutrality was widely criticized as a failure of leadership and a tacit endorsement of systemic racism within law enforcement agencies.

In the context of refugee crises and forced displacement, political neutrality among governments and international organizations can perpetuate human suffering and exacerbate humanitarian emergencies. During the Syrian refugee crisis, some countries adopted a neutral stance or closed their borders to refugees, citing concerns about national security or domestic stability. However, this neutrality effectively denied asylum to vulnerable individuals fleeing conflict and persecution, contributing to overcrowded refugee camps and a lack of access to essential services.

In the realm of international diplomacy, neutrality in the face of geopolitical conflicts can hinder efforts towards peacebuilding and conflict resolution. The ongoing conflict between Israel and Palestine exemplifies how political neutrality among world powers has failed to address the root causes of the conflict and alleviate the suffering of civilians caught in the crossfire. Despite repeated calls for a neutral mediator to facilitate negotiations, entrenched political interests and power dynamics have hindered progress towards a lasting peace agreement.

Neutrality and Complicity

Political neutrality can also serve as a guide for complicity, allowing individuals or institutions to avoid accountability for their actions or lack thereof. By claiming neutrality, policymakers may absolve themselves of responsibility for addressing injustices or upholding human rights, effectively enabling the perpetuation of systemic inequalities. This complicity in maintaining the status quo can have far-reaching consequences for marginalized communities and undermine efforts towards social justice and equity.

In authoritarian regimes or repressive political environments, neutrality among government officials and institutions often translates into complicity with human rights abuses and authoritarian rule. For instance, in countries like Belarus, where political dissent is met with harsh repression and violence, government officials who claim neutrality or refuse to take a stand against human rights violations effectively enable the regime's authoritarian grip on power. By failing to condemn or intervene in systemic abuses, they become complicit in the erosion of democratic norms and the suppression of fundamental freedoms.

In the context of corporate governance, neutrality among business leaders and executives can enable unethical practices and exploitation of workers and communities. The Rana Plaza factory collapse in Bangladesh in 2013, which resulted in the deaths of over 1,100 garment workers, highlighted the complicity of multinational corporations and fashion brands in perpetuating unsafe working conditions and labour rights abuses. Despite warnings about structural deficiencies in the building and concerns raised by labour rights activists, many companies remained neutral or indifferent to the plight of garment workers, prioritizing profit over worker safety.

In authoritarian regimes or repressive political environments, neutrality among media organizations and journalists can facilitate government censorship and propaganda. The case of Jamal Khashoggi, a Saudi Arabian journalist and dissident who was brutally murdered in the Saudi consulate in Istanbul in 2018, illustrates how political neutrality can have deadly consequences for those who challenge authoritarian rule. Despite mounting evidence implicating the Saudi government in Khashoggi's killing, some media outlets adopted a neutral stance or refrained from condemning the regime's actions, fearing reprisals or jeopardizing diplomatic relations.

Let me quote yet another example Sergei Magnitsky was a Russian lawyer who uncovered a massive corruption scheme involving Russian officials. He investigated and exposed the theft of $230 million from the Russian government, implicating high-ranking officials and organized crime figures. Instead of being hailed as a whistle-blower, Magnitsky faced severe repercussions for his actions.

In 2008, Magnitsky was arrested by the very officials he had accused of corruption. He was held in pretrial detention for almost a year under harsh conditions, denied medical treatment, and eventually died in custody in 2009 at the age of 37. His death was attributed to medical neglect and abuse.

Magnitsky's case highlights the deadly consequences that can befall individuals who challenge authoritarian rule even when they attempt to remain politically neutral in their actions. Magnitsky was simply doing his job as a lawyer and accountant, investigating financial fraud, without any overt political agenda. However, his findings threatened powerful interests within the Russian government and led to his persecution and ultimately his tragic death.

The case of Sergei Magnitsky has become a symbol of the dangers faced by those who attempt to uphold the rule of law and expose corruption in authoritarian regimes. It underscores how even neutrality and professionalism in pursuing justice can be perceived as a threat by authoritarian rulers who prioritize their own power and interests above all else.

Let's see one more incident in India. Narendra Dabholkar was a prominent Indian rationalist and social activist who campaigned against superstition and black magic. He was the founder of the Maharashtra Andhashraddha Nirmoolan Samiti (MANS), an organization dedicated to eradicating superstition and promoting scientific temper.

Dabholkar's work and activism often brought him into conflict with religious extremists and practitioners of superstitions, who viewed his efforts as a threat to their beliefs and practices. Despite his efforts to remain politically neutral and focused on scientific education and social reform, Dabholkar became a target.

On August 20, 2013, Narendra Dabholkar was shot dead by two assailants while he was out for a morning walk in Pune, Maharashtra. His assassination shocked the nation and highlighted the dangers faced by activists who challenge entrenched beliefs and practices in a society where political and religious interests are often intertwined.

Dabholkar's murder sparked widespread outrage and calls for justice. It also prompted debates about the safety of activists and the need to protect freedom of speech and expression in India. His death underscored the risks faced by individuals who advocate for rationalism and social reform in the face of opposition from powerful interests, including those with authoritarian tendencies.

The case of Narendra Dabholkar serves as a sobering reminder of how political neutrality and commitment to social causes can lead to deadly consequences in environments where authoritarianism seeks to suppress dissent and maintain control over public discourse.

Impact of Neutrality on Policy-making and Social Progress

Neutrality in politics and governance can significantly impact policy-making processes and hinder progress towards social justice and equality. When policymakers prioritize neutrality over advocacy and decisive action, they may perpetuate existing disparities and marginalize vulnerable populations. Moreover, neutrality can impede the implementation of transformative policies aimed at addressing systemic injustices and advancing the common good.

In debates over climate change policy, political neutrality among lawmakers and government officials has contributed to delays in adopting comprehensive measures to mitigate the impacts of global warming. Despite overwhelming scientific evidence pointing to the urgency of addressing climate change, political gridlock and inertia driven by neutrality have hindered efforts to enact meaningful legislation and transition to renewable energy sources. As a result, marginalized communities disproportionately bear the brunt of environmental degradation and climate-related disasters, exacerbating existing inequalities.

In the realm of healthcare policy, neutrality among policymakers and healthcare institutions can hinder efforts to address public health crises and disparities in healthcare access. The opioid epidemic in the United States, which has claimed thousands of lives due to overdose deaths and addiction, illustrates how political neutrality and industry influence have delayed regulatory action and impeded efforts to combat the crisis. Pharmaceutical companies that produce and market opioids have lobbied for leniency and opposed stricter regulations, while policymakers have been slow to enact comprehensive measures to address addiction and improve access to treatment.

In the domain of LGBTQ+ rights and equality, political neutrality among lawmakers and government officials can perpetuate discrimination and undermine efforts towards inclusion and social acceptance. The lack of comprehensive anti-discrimination laws protecting LGBTQ+ individuals in many countries reflects the failure of political leaders to prioritize equality and human rights. Despite growing public support for LGBTQ+ rights, political neutrality and opposition from conservative groups have stalled progress towards achieving full legal recognition and protection for LGBTQ+ individuals.

The paradox of neutrality in politics and governance reveals the inherent tension between impartiality and accountability, between maintaining the status quo and advancing social progress. While political neutrality may be touted as a virtue of democratic governance, it can often lead to inaction, complicity, and the perpetuation of systemic injustices. By recognizing the limitations of neutrality and advocating for ethical leadership and decisive action, policymakers can work towards a more just and equitable society, where neutrality is not an excuse for indifference, but a commitment to upholding human rights and dignity for all.

18

Neutrality in Business and Corporate Culture

"When we choose neutrality, we choose to stand on the wrong side of history"

- Unknown

Neutrality in business and corporate culture is often perceived as a stance of impartiality and objectivity, yet it can paradoxically perpetuate systemic inequalities, workplace harassment, and unethical practices. This exploration delves into the complexities of neutrality within corporate environments, examining its implications for organizational culture, employee well-being, and ethical conduct. Through suitable examples, incidents, and events, we illuminate the nuanced dynamics of neutrality in shaping business practices and perpetuating harmful norms.

Neutrality and Systemic Inequalities

In hiring and promotion practices, corporate neutrality can reinforce systemic biases and discrimination against marginalized groups. Despite initiatives aimed at promoting diversity and inclusion, many companies maintain a neutral stance in recruitment and advancement decisions, resulting in the underrepresentation of women, minorities, and individuals from disadvantaged backgrounds in leadership positions. The tech industry, for instance, has faced criticism for its predominantly male and homogeneous workforce, reflecting the perpetuation of systemic inequalities in hiring and retention practices.

In compensation and pay equity, corporate neutrality can lead to disparities in wages and benefits based on gender, race, or other demographic factors. Despite legal mandates and public scrutiny, many companies fail to address pay gaps and inequities within their organizations, citing a commitment to market forces and meritocracy. However, this neutrality effectively perpetuates systemic inequalities and denies equal opportunities for advancement and economic security to marginalized employees.

Neutrality and Workplace Harassment

In addressing workplace harassment and discrimination, corporate neutrality can create a culture of silence and impunity, allowing perpetrators to evade accountability and victims to suffer in silence. The #MeToo movement brought to light numerous cases of sexual harassment and misconduct in corporate settings, exposing the prevalence of toxic workplace cultures where neutrality and complicity enabled abusive behaviour to persist unchecked. Despite growing awareness and public outcry, some companies remained neutral or indifferent to allegations of harassment, prioritizing reputation management over employee well-being.

In whistleblowing and reporting mechanisms, corporate neutrality can deter employees from coming forward with concerns about misconduct or unethical behaviour. Fear of retaliation, ostracism, or career repercussions often dissuades individuals from speaking out against wrongdoing, leading to a culture of silence and complicity within organizations. The Volkswagen emissions scandal, where employees who raised concerns about fraudulent emissions tests were ignored or marginalized, illustrates how corporate neutrality can thwart efforts to expose corporate malfeasance and hold decision-makers accountable.

Neutrality and Unethical Practices

In supply chain management and corporate responsibility, neutrality can enable unethical practices and human rights abuses in global supply chains. Despite commitments to ethical sourcing and sustainability, many companies turn a blind eye to labour violations and environmental degradation in their supply chains, citing a desire to remain neutral in complex geopolitical and economic contexts. The Rana Plaza factory collapse in Bangladesh, where over 1,100 garment workers died due to unsafe working conditions, exposed the complicity of multinational corporations in perpetuating exploitative labour practices through their pursuit of cost-saving measures and neutrality in oversight.

In lobbying and political influence, corporate neutrality can undermine democratic governance and regulatory oversight, allowing powerful corporations to shape policy outcomes in their favour. The influence of corporate lobbying on environmental regulations, tax policies, and consumer protections often tilts the playing field in favour of vested interests, compromising the public interest and perpetuating systemic inequalities.

The Citizens United Supreme Court decision in the United States, which granted corporations the same free speech rights as individuals and unleashed a flood of corporate money into political campaigns, exemplifies how neutrality in campaign finance laws can distort democratic processes and undermine public trust in government. In an electoral bond case before the apex court of India, a parallel argument was presented, asserting that corporates contributing to political parties in India have rights akin to citizens' rights to information, emphasizing the importance of maintaining secrecy.

Neutrality and Environmental Impact

In corporate sustainability efforts, neutrality can lead to greenwashing and superficial commitments to environmental stewardship. Despite public pledges to reduce carbon emissions and mitigate environmental impact, some companies engage in tokenistic gestures and PR campaigns to project an image of neutrality and eco-friendliness. However, behind the facade of sustainability, these companies may continue to prioritize profit over environmental responsibility, perpetuating ecological harm and contributing to climate change.

In the extraction and exploitation of natural resources, corporate neutrality can facilitate environmental degradation and land displacement in communities around the world. The case of the Dakota Access Pipeline (DAPL) in the United States, where Energy Transfer Partners sought to construct an oil pipeline through Native

American lands and water sources, illustrates how corporate neutrality can enable the violation of indigenous rights and environmental destruction. Despite protests and legal challenges from indigenous activists and environmentalists, the company maintained a neutral stance, prioritizing financial interests over environmental and social concerns.

Neutrality and Corporate Governance

In corporate governance and boardroom dynamics, neutrality can perpetuate gender imbalance and lack of diversity among decision-makers. Despite calls for greater representation of women and minorities on corporate boards, many companies remain neutral or resistant to diversity initiatives, citing a commitment to meritocracy and neutrality in selection processes. As a result, women and minority groups continue to be underrepresented in leadership positions, contributing to a lack of diverse perspectives and equitable decision-making within organizations.

In corporate social responsibility (CSR) initiatives, neutrality can result in superficial philanthropy and detached engagement with social issues. Some companies may engage in one-off charitable donations or community projects to project an image of neutrality and corporate citizenship, without addressing the root causes of social problems or systemic injustices. This approach, known as "check book philanthropy," allows companies to maintain a neutral stance while avoiding meaningful engagement with stakeholders and societal challenges.

Let me explain a classic example that exemplifies the concept of "check book philanthropy" and the superficial engagement in corporate social responsibility (CSR) initiatives is the case of Nike in the 1990s regarding labour practices in its supply chain.

During the 1990s, Nike faced widespread criticism for its labour practices in developing countries, particularly concerning sweatshop conditions and low wages paid to workers manufacturing its products. This scrutiny brought significant public and media attention, questioning Nike's commitment to ethical labour practices and CSR.

In response to these criticisms, Nike initially engaged in what appeared to be CSR initiatives aimed at improving labour conditions. They launched programs like the "Nike Fair Labour Association," which included audits and reports on factory conditions. On the surface, these initiatives seemed to demonstrate a commitment to addressing social issues within its supply chain.

However, critics argued that Nike's approach was largely focused on superficial measures and "check book philanthropy." While the company did make charitable donations and implemented some improvements in factory conditions, it was accused of avoiding addressing the systemic issues of low wages, harsh working conditions, and lack of worker rights that persisted in its supply chain.

Neutrality and Supply Chain Ethics

In global supply chains, neutrality can perpetuate labour exploitation and human rights abuses in manufacturing and production processes. Despite commitments to ethical sourcing and responsible supply chain management, many companies turn a blind eye to violations of labour rights and worker safety in factories and sweatshops overseas. The collapse of the Rana Plaza factory in Bangladesh, where workers were forced to toil in unsafe conditions for low wages, exposed the complicity of multinational corporations in perpetuating exploitative labour practices through their pursuit of cost-saving measures and neutrality in oversight.

In the technology industry, neutrality in supply chain management can enable the proliferation of conflict minerals and human rights abuses in the extraction of raw materials. Companies that manufacture electronic devices often source minerals such as coltan, cobalt, and gold from regions plagued by armed conflict and exploitation, such as the Democratic Republic of Congo. Despite awareness of the ethical concerns surrounding conflict minerals, some technology companies maintain a neutral stance in their supply chain practices, prioritizing cost efficiency and supply chain continuity over ethical considerations.

The ramifications of neutrality in business and corporate culture extend beyond mere indifference, encompassing environmental degradation, governance failures, and human rights abuses. By examining real-world examples and incidents, we gain insight into the pervasive impact of neutrality on organizational behaviour and societal outcomes. To address these challenges, companies must move beyond neutrality and embrace ethical leadership, transparency, and accountability in their business practices, fostering a culture of integrity, responsibility, and respect for all stakeholders.

19

Neutrality and Social Justice Movements

"He who stands neutral is under the blackest of suspicions"

- Edward Bulwer-Lytton

Neutrality in the context of social justice movements presents a complex and contentious dilemma. While neutrality may be perceived as a stance of impartiality and objectivity, it can often perpetuate systemic inequalities and hinder progress towards meaningful social change. This exploration delves into the tensions between neutrality and activism, examining the consequences of remaining neutral in the face of discrimination, oppression, and injustice. Through examples, incidents, and global events, we illuminate the nuanced dynamics of neutrality within social justice movements and its impact on marginalized communities.

Tensions Between Neutrality and Activism

In the realm of racial justice, neutrality among individuals and institutions can contribute to the perpetuation of systemic racism and inequities. The Black Lives Matter (BLM) movement, which emerged in response to police brutality and racial injustice against Black communities, has highlighted the limitations of neutrality in addressing systemic racism. While some individuals may claim neutrality to avoid taking a stand on contentious issues, such as police violence and racial profiling, this neutrality effectively reinforces the status quo and undermines efforts towards racial equity and justice.

In the fight for LGBTQ+ rights and equality, neutrality among policymakers and lawmakers can impede progress towards legislative protections and societal acceptance. Despite increasing public support for LGBTQ+ rights, some politicians may adopt a neutral stance on issues such as marriage equality and transgender rights, citing personal beliefs or political expediency. However, this neutrality effectively denies equal rights and protections to LGBTQ+ individuals, perpetuating discrimination and marginalization within society.

In the realm of indigenous rights and land sovereignty, neutrality among governments and corporations can perpetuate colonial legacies and land dispossession.

Indigenous-led movements, such as the Standing Rock protests against the Dakota Access Pipeline in the United States, have faced opposition from entities claiming a neutral stance or prioritizing economic interests over indigenous sovereignty. Despite indigenous communities' calls for land protection and consultation, neutrality from decision-makers has enabled the violation of indigenous rights and environmental destruction.

In the disability rights movement, neutrality among policymakers and public institutions can hinder efforts to promote accessibility and inclusivity. Despite legal mandates such as the Americans with Disabilities Act (ADA) in the United States, many public spaces and services remain inaccessible to individuals with disabilities due to a lack of enforcement and political will. Neutrality in addressing accessibility barriers effectively perpetuates discrimination and exclusion, denying people with disabilities equal opportunities and participation in society.

Consequences of Remaining Neutral

In the context of gender equality and women's rights, neutrality among employers and corporate leaders can perpetuate gender discrimination and workplace inequities. Despite efforts to promote diversity and inclusion, some companies may maintain a neutral stance on issues such as pay equity and maternity leave, failing to address systemic barriers to gender equality in the workplace. This neutrality effectively side-lines the voices and experiences of women, contributing to disparities in pay, promotion, and leadership opportunities.

In the global response to climate change, neutrality among governments and policymakers can exacerbate environmental degradation and social injustice. Despite the urgency of addressing climate change, some countries may adopt a neutral stance on climate action, prioritizing economic interests and fossil fuel industries over environmental sustainability and social welfare. This neutrality effectively perpetuates environmental injustices and disproportionately impacts marginalized communities, who bear the brunt of climate-related disasters and resource depletion.

In the context of refugee and migrant rights, neutrality among countries and international organizations can exacerbate humanitarian crises and violate human rights. The European migrant crisis, characterized by mass displacement and forced migration, highlighted the consequences of European countries adopting a neutral stance or implementing restrictive immigration policies. This neutrality effectively denied asylum to refugees fleeing conflict and persecution, contributing to overcrowded refugee camps and human rights abuses at borders.

In the realm of economic justice and income inequality, neutrality among policymakers and financial institutions can perpetuate wealth disparities and social stratification. Despite growing awareness of wealth concentration and corporate influence in politics, some governments maintain a neutral stance on tax policies and economic reforms that address income inequality. This neutrality effectively protects the interests of the wealthy elite while exacerbating poverty and social injustice for marginalized communities.

The Rohingya refugee crisis in Myanmar, where hundreds of thousands of Rohingya Muslims were forced to flee violence and persecution, illustrates the consequences of international neutrality in the face of human rights abuses. Despite widespread condemnation of the Myanmar government's atrocities, some countries maintained a neutral stance or refrained from taking decisive action to hold perpetrators accountable. This neutrality effectively enabled the perpetuation of ethnic cleansing and human rights violations against the Rohingya population.

The global response to the COVID-19 pandemic underscored the importance of collective action and solidarity in addressing public health crises. However, neutrality among governments and international organizations in distributing vaccines and resources has led to disparities in access and vaccine inequity. While some countries have prioritized vaccine distribution and supported global vaccination efforts, others have adopted a neutral stance or prioritized national interests, exacerbating health disparities and prolonging the pandemic's impact on vulnerable populations.

The global response to the Black Lives Matter protests following the murder of George Floyd in 2020 revealed the consequences of institutional neutrality in addressing systemic racism and police violence. While millions took to the streets to demand racial justice and police reform, some political leaders and law enforcement agencies maintained a neutral stance or responded with violence and repression. This neutrality effectively perpetuated racial disparities in policing and criminal justice, undermining efforts towards accountability and systemic change.

The *#MeToo* movement, which gained momentum in 2017 with women sharing their experiences of sexual harassment and assault, exposed the consequences of organizational neutrality in addressing workplace harassment and gender-based violence. Despite widespread awareness of the prevalence of harassment and discrimination, many companies and institutions initially responded with neutrality or token gestures, failing to implement comprehensive policies and accountability mechanisms. This neutrality effectively silenced survivors and perpetuated cultures of impunity, hindering progress towards gender equality and workplace safety.

The tensions between neutrality and activism within social justice movements underscore the complexities of navigating moral dilemmas and advocating for change. By examining the consequences of remaining neutral in the fight against discrimination, oppression, and injustice, we gain insight into the urgency of taking a stand and challenging systemic inequalities. Moving forward, individuals, institutions, and governments must recognize the limitations of neutrality and prioritize ethical leadership, solidarity, and collective action in the pursuit of social justice and equity for all members of society.

Moreover, within social justice movements, the tensions between neutrality and activism serve as a poignant reminder of the moral imperative to stand on the right side of history. Inaction in the face of injustice not only perpetuates harm but also undermines the very essence of these movements. Therefore, it is incumbent upon each of us to actively engage in critical reflection, to interrogate our privileges, and to use our voices and platforms to amplify marginalized perspectives. By recognizing the interconnectedness of our struggles and fostering genuine empathy and solidarity, we can build a more inclusive and equitable world where neutrality is not an option, but rather an active commitment to justice and human dignity.

Moreover, fostering a culture that values diversity and actively promotes inclusivity requires continuous effort and courage. Each act of solidarity, no matter how small, contributes to the collective momentum towards a society where justice and equality prevail over indifference and silence. Thus, by embracing our roles as advocates for change, we fulfil our duty to create a future where all voices are heard and valued.

Ethical Dilemmas and Challenges of Neutrality

From exploring its implications to addressing the consequences of inaction and reshaping the neutrality paradigm

20

Unravelling the Ethical Implications of Neutrality

"Neutrality is the language of privilege, spoken by those who can afford to ignore injustice"

- Unknown

Let's unpack the idea of neutrality—a term that often sounds fair and balanced but can actually hide some pretty shady stuff, letting oppressors off the hook. In this chapter, we're going on a journey to explore the ethics of neutrality, uncovering how it can be used to shield the bad guys from scrutiny and let injustice thrive. We'll dive into historical tales, ponder some big questions, and look at what's happening today to understand how neutrality isn't always what it seems.

Historical Instances: Neutrality as an Enabler of Oppression

Throughout history, neutrality has played a pivotal role in facilitating the rise and sustenance of oppressive regimes.

Switzerland during World War II

Switzerland's neutrality during the Second World War is a prime example of how a nation's purported impartiality can mask complicity. While Switzerland avoided direct involvement in the conflict, its banks served as a safe haven for Nazi plundered wealth. Jewish assets stolen by the Nazis, including gold extracted from victims of the Holocaust, found their way into Swiss banks. Despite knowledge of these transactions, Swiss authorities remained passive, allowing the financial system to thrive while turning a blind eye to the horrors of the Holocaust.

The Spanish Civil War and International Non-Intervention

The Spanish Civil War (1936-1939) saw the rise of General Francisco Franco's fascist forces, supported by Nazi Germany and Fascist Italy. Despite the clear violation of human rights and democratic principles, major powers such as Britain, France, and the United States opted for a policy of non-intervention. This neutrality effectively enabled Franco's victory, prolonging the suffering of those fighting for democracy and leading to decades of authoritarian rule in Spain.

Moral Neutrality: Evading Responsibility in the Face of Injustice

The concept of "moral neutrality" emerges as a troubling phenomenon wherein individuals or institutions abstain from taking a moral stance under the guise of impartiality. By adopting a neutral position, actors may evade accountability for addressing ethical wrongs, effectively legitimizing oppression through their silence. Consider the case of corporations operating in authoritarian regimes, choosing to maintain neutrality to safeguard profits while turning a blind eye to human rights abuses inflicted upon workers or local communities. In such scenarios, neutrality becomes a convenient shield, allowing complicity to masquerade as impartiality.

Corporate Complicity in Authoritarian Regimes

Numerous multinational corporations operating in authoritarian states have faced accusations of complicity in human rights abuses due to their adherence to a stance of neutrality. For example, tech giants like Google and Apple have come under scrutiny for complying with censorship laws in countries like China, effectively enabling state repression and silencing dissident voices in exchange for market access and profit.

Financial Institutions and Social Responsibility

Banks and financial institutions often claim neutrality when faced with ethically contentious issues such as fossil fuel investments or financing for controversial projects. For instance, major banks have provided funding for environmentally destructive ventures like coal mining or oil pipelines while maintaining a facade of neutrality, absolving themselves of responsibility for the ecological and social consequences of their investments.

Leveraging Neutrality to Maintain the Status Quo

Powerful institutions, whether governmental bodies, media conglomerates, or religious organizations, often wield neutrality as a tool to preserve the status quo and suppress dissent. By positioning themselves as neutral arbiters, these entities may manipulate public discourse, silencing marginalized voices and perpetuating existing power structures. In media coverage, for instance, the phenomenon of false balance presents a stark illustration of neutrality gone awry, as news outlets equate fact with opinion, providing undue legitimacy to fringe viewpoints and undermining efforts to confront systemic injustices.

Media False Balance and the Climate Crisis

In the realm of media coverage, the phenomenon of false balance has had devastating consequences, particularly in the context of climate change. News outlets, in an attempt to appear impartial, have often presented the scientifically established reality of anthropogenic climate change as debatable, providing undue platform to climate change deniers. This false balance not only distorts public perception but also impedes meaningful action on mitigating the climate crisis, perpetuating environmental degradation for the sake of perceived neutrality.

Religious Institutions and Social Justice

Religious organizations, while professing neutrality in matters of politics, frequently find themselves entangled in debates over social justice issues such as LGBTQ+ rights or reproductive rights. By maintaining neutrality or purported neutrality on these issues, religious institutions may inadvertently uphold discriminatory practices or contribute to the marginalization of vulnerable communities, failing to live up to their professed values of compassion and equality.

By weaving together these examples and incidents, we gain a deeper understanding of how neutrality, far from being a benign concept, can serve as a shield for the oppressor, perpetuating injustice and evading ethical responsibility. Whether through historical instances of national neutrality enabling fascist regimes, corporate complicity in human rights abuses, or media false balance distorting public discourse, the ethical implications of neutrality are manifold and profound.

Moving forward, it is essential to critically examine the role of neutrality in our societal structures and to strive for a more nuanced understanding that prioritizes justice, equity, and human dignity over the illusion of impartiality.

21

Cost of Inaction: When Neutrality Breeds Apathy

"Neutrality is the refuge of cowards and the excuse of the indifferent"

- Unknown

Let's talk about neutrality—a concept that often gets painted as fair and balanced, but can actually have some serious consequences when it's the go-to response to big social and political issues. In this chapter, we're going to dive deep into what happens when we choose to stay neutral, exploring how it can lead to apathy, weaken social bonds, and hold us back from making positive changes together. We'll use examples from psychology and real life to understand just how damaging neutrality can be to our communities and progress as a society.

The Bystander Effect: Why We Stay Silent

Ever heard of the bystander effect? It's a psychological thing that shows how we're less likely to help out in an emergency if we think someone else will do it. This idea of "diffusion of responsibility" means we might hold back from speaking up or taking action when we see something wrong, just because we think someone else will step in.

The bystander effect, a well-documented psychological phenomenon, highlights how individuals are less likely to intervene in emergency situations when others are present. This phenomenon, characterized by diffusion of responsibility and social influence, offers insights into the inertia that often accompanies widespread neutrality. By assuming that others will take action or by conforming to the perceived norms of inaction, individuals may refrain from speaking out or getting involved in addressing pressing issues, perpetuating a cycle of apathy and indifference.

Psychological Mechanisms

The bystander effect is driven by several psychological mechanisms, including diffusion of responsibility, social influence, and pluralistic ignorance. Individuals may feel less personally responsible for taking action when others are present, assuming that someone else will intervene.

Additionally, the presence of others can influence individuals to conform to perceived social norms of inaction, leading to a collective paralysis even in situations where help is needed urgently.

Case Studies

Famous incidents such as the murder of Kitty Genovese in 1964, where numerous bystanders witnessed the attack but failed to intervene or call for help, illustrate the chilling impact of the bystander effect. Despite the clear need for assistance, the diffusion of responsibility among onlookers resulted in tragic consequences during the civil rights movement in the United States or the violence against African Americans in the South during the 1950s and 1960s. Similarly, studies have shown that the bystander effect is not limited to physical emergencies but also extends to instances of social injustice, where individuals may refrain from speaking out or intervening due to social pressures or the belief that others will take action.

Erosion of Social Solidarity: What Happens When We Don't Stand Together

When neutrality becomes the norm, it can break down the bonds that hold us together as a society. Take racial profiling or police brutality, for example. When people see these things happening but choose to stay quiet, it doesn't just let the injustice continue—it also weakens the trust and unity we need to make things better for everyone

Consider the case of bystanders who witness instances of racial profiling or police brutality but choose to remain silent. Their neutrality not only fails to challenge systemic injustice but also undermines the trust and cohesion necessary for meaningful social change.

Social Fragmentation

When neutrality becomes the dominant response to social injustice, it can fragment communities and weaken the bonds of empathy and solidarity that underpin collective action. The erosion of social solidarity perpetuates cycles of marginalization and oppression, as individuals feel isolated or powerless to challenge systemic injustices. This fragmentation can be particularly pronounced in diverse societies where different groups may have divergent experiences and perspectives on issues of inequality and discrimination.

Historical Precedents

Throughout history, movements for social change have been fuelled by collective solidarity and a shared commitment to justice. Conversely, periods of societal stagnation or regression often coincide with a lack of solidarity and widespread neutrality in the face of injustice.

For example, the civil rights movement in the United States drew strength from grassroots activism and solidarity across racial lines, challenging entrenched systems of segregation and discrimination. In contrast, periods of social apathy and division, such as the post-Reconstruction era or the rise of authoritarian regimes, have been marked by the erosion of social solidarity and the normalization of neutrality.

Contributing to a Culture of Cynicism: Why We Lose Hope

If neutrality is everywhere, it can make us feel like nothing we do will make a difference. Neutrality, when pervasive in societal discourse, can contribute to a culture of cynicism and disengagement with important social and political issues. When individuals perceive neutrality as the default response to contentious issues, they may become disillusioned with the possibility of effecting change through collective action. This cynicism and disengagement are exacerbated by the proliferation of misinformation and polarization in media and online spaces, where neutrality is often equated with objectivity, leading to public scepticism and withdrawal from civic participation.

The Global Refugee Crisis

In the face of the largest refugee crisis since World War II, many countries have adopted a stance of neutrality or closed their borders, citing concerns over security or economic strain. This collective inaction not only exacerbates the suffering of displaced populations but also reflects a broader lack of global solidarity and cooperation in addressing humanitarian emergencies.

Silence on Climate Change

Despite overwhelming scientific consensus on the urgency of addressing climate change, political leaders and individuals alike often adopt a stance of neutrality or ambivalence, failing to take decisive action to mitigate environmental degradation. This collective inertia not only jeopardizes the future of the planet but also reflects complacency and reluctance to confront uncomfortable truths.

Online Disinformation and Neutrality

In the realm of social media, algorithms designed to prioritize engagement often amplify sensationalist content and polarizing viewpoints, while downplaying nuanced or balanced perspectives. This algorithmic neutrality perpetuates echo chambers and reinforces existing biases, contributing to a culture of cynicism and disengagement with important social and political issues.

Media Literacy and Critical Thinking

Addressing the culture of cynicism and disengagement requires a multifaceted approach that includes media literacy education and the cultivation of critical thinking skills. By empowering individuals to critically evaluate information and recognize the biases inherent in media narratives, we can counteract the spread of misinformation and polarization that perpetuate neutrality as a default response to complex issues.

Community Building and Grassroots Organizing

Building resilient communities and fostering grassroots organizing can serve as antidotes to the culture of cynicism and disengagement. By creating spaces for dialogue, collaboration, and collective action, communities can counteract feelings of isolation and apathy, empowering individuals to channel their concerns into meaningful social change. Examples of successful community-based initiatives, such as neighbourhood watch programs or mutual aid networks, demonstrate the power of solidarity and collective action in addressing local challenges and fostering a sense of agency and belonging.

By further exploring the psychological mechanisms underlying the bystander effect, examining historical precedents of social solidarity and fragmentation, and highlighting strategies for combating cynicism and disengagement, we gain a more nuanced understanding of the complex interplay between neutrality, apathy, and societal dynamics. Through concerted efforts to challenge indifference, cultivate solidarity, and promote active citizenship, we can work towards a more just and equitable society built on empathy, compassion, and collective action.

The cost of inaction in the face of critical issues is steep, and neutrality, far from being a neutral stance, can breed apathy, erode social solidarity, and foster a culture of cynicism and disengagement. By understanding the psychological underpinnings of the bystander effect and examining real-world examples of collective neutrality, we gain insights into the profound societal consequences of indifference. Moving forward, it is imperative to challenge the status quo of neutrality and cultivate a culture of active citizenship, empathy, and solidarity in the pursuit of a more just and equitable society.

22

Challenging the Neutrality Paradigm

"Neutrality, as a lasting principle, is an evidence of weakness"

- Lajos Kossuth

et's talk about neutrality—a concept often seen as fair and balanced, but it's not always the best approach when it comes to tackling big social and political issues. In this discussion, we're going to explore some different ways of thinking that put justice, fairness, and accountability front and centre. We'll look at examples from around the world to see how we can make for a paradigm shift towards active engagement and advocacy for positive change.

Moving Beyond Neutrality

Making Justice a Priority

Instead of striving for neutrality, decision-makers should prioritize justice as a guiding principle. This entails actively considering the impact of policies and actions on marginalized communities and addressing underlying power imbalances.

Restorative justice practices, which focus on repairing harm and restoring relationships rather than punitive measures, offer an alternative approach to traditional legal systems. Restorative justice processes empower victims and offenders to participate in dialogue and reconciliation, fostering accountability and healing within communities.

Focusing on Equity

Embracing equity requires recognizing and addressing systemic barriers that perpetuate inequality and discrimination. Rather than maintaining a neutral stance, institutions should actively work to dismantle oppressive structures and create opportunities for marginalized groups to thrive

Affirmative action policies in education and employment aim to address historical inequities by providing preferential treatment to underrepresented groups. While controversial, these policies seek to level the playing field and promote diversity and inclusion in traditionally homogenous environments.

Holding Ourselves Accountable

Upholding accountability is essential for ensuring that individuals and institutions are held responsible for their actions and decisions. Transparency in decision-making processes fosters trust and enables stakeholders to hold decision-makers accountable for their actions.

Whistle-blower protections and mechanisms for reporting misconduct are essential for promoting accountability within organizations. Whistle-blowers play a crucial role in exposing wrongdoing and holding powerful entities accountable, even in the face of retaliation and personal risk.

Understanding Intersectionality

Recognizing the interconnected nature of oppression and privilege, intersectional justice centres the experiences of marginalized individuals and addresses multiple forms of discrimination simultaneously.

The Black feminist movement, led by activists such as Kimberlé Crenshaw and Audre Lorde, emphasizes the importance of intersectionality in understanding and addressing the unique challenges faced by Black women. By highlighting the intersections of race, gender, class, and other identities, intersectional feminism challenges traditional approaches to social justice and advocates for inclusive, intersectional solutions.

Decolonizing Our Thinking

Decolonizing approaches seek to challenge colonial legacies and centre indigenous knowledge, perspectives, and sovereignty in decision-making processes.

The Idle No More movement, initiated by indigenous activists in Canada in 2012, mobilized indigenous and non-indigenous allies in protests, teach-ins, and direct actions to resist colonial policies and protect indigenous land and water rights. By foregrounding indigenous sovereignty and decolonization, Idle No More challenged the neutrality of government policies and demanded meaningful Indigenous self-determination.

Participatory Democracy

Participatory democracy promotes inclusive decision-making processes that actively involve affected communities in shaping policies and initiatives that impact their lives.

Participatory budgeting initiatives, such as those implemented in cities like Porto Alegre, Brazil, and New York City, empower residents to directly participate in allocating public funds and prioritizing community projects. By decentralizing decision-making power and amplifying marginalized voices, participatory democracy challenges the neutrality of traditional top-down governance structures and fosters greater accountability and transparency.

Strategies for Promoting Critical Thinking and Ethical Decision-Making

Education for Empowerment

Empowering individuals with critical thinking skills and ethical awareness is essential for challenging the status quo and advocating for change. Education systems should prioritize teaching students to critically evaluate information, question assumptions, and recognize their role in promoting social justice.

Critical pedagogy approaches, such as those advocated by Brazilian educator Paulo Freire, emphasize dialogue, reflection, and action as transformative tools for addressing social inequalities. By engaging students in critical discussions about power dynamics and oppression, educators can empower them to become agents of change in their communities.

Leading by Example

Promoting ethical leadership requires nurturing a culture of integrity, accountability, and moral courage within organizations and communities. Leaders must prioritize ethical considerations in decision-making processes and model ethical behaviour for others to follow.

The ethical leadership demonstrated by figures such as Mahatma Gandhi, Nelson Mandela, and Malala Yousafzai serves as inspiration for individuals and communities striving for positive change. These leaders exemplify the principles of integrity, empathy, and social justice in their actions and inspire others to do the same.

It may be pertinent to recall the words of Mahatma Gandhi, Martin Luther King Jr. and Malala Yousafzai here:

"Silence becomes cowardice when occasion demands speaking out the whole truth and acting accordingly"

- Mahatma Gandhi

"We realize the importance of our voices only when we are silenced"

- Malala Yousafzai

"In the end, we will remember not the words of our enemies, but the silence of our friends. Our lives begin to end the day we become silent about things that matter"

-Martin Luther King Jr.

Getting Involved

Active civic engagement is essential for challenging the neutrality paradigm and advocating for systemic change. Individuals can participate in grassroots movements, community organizing, and advocacy efforts to amplify marginalized voices and advance social justice agendas.

The global climate justice movement, led by activists such as Greta Thunberg and the youth-led organization Fridays for Future, demonstrates the power of grassroots mobilization in demanding urgent action on climate change. By organizing strikes, protests, and direct actions, activists have pressured governments and corporations to prioritize climate justice and sustainability.

Media Literacy and Information Literacy

Promoting media literacy and information literacy equips individuals with the skills to critically evaluate sources of information, discern bias, and recognize misinformation and disinformation.

The spread of misinformation and conspiracy theories during the COVID-19 pandemic highlighted the importance of media literacy in combating false narratives and promoting evidence-based information. Initiatives such as fact-checking organizations, media literacy programs in schools, and public awareness campaigns play a crucial role in promoting critical thinking and countering misinformation.

Building Ethical Leaders

Investing in ethical leadership development programs and mentorship opportunities cultivates a new generation of leaders committed to integrity, accountability, and social justice. Let me quote a few;

The Mandela Washington Fellowship for Young African Leaders, initiated by the U.S. Department of State, provides leadership training, networking opportunities, and mentorship to emerging leaders from across Africa. By equipping fellows with skills and knowledge to address pressing social challenges in their communities, the fellowship promotes ethical leadership and civic engagement on the continent.

The Aspen Institute's Henry Crown Fellowship: This fellowship program in the United States selects emerging leaders and provides them with a transformative experience to develop their leadership abilities. It emphasizes values-based leadership and encourages fellows to address societal issues with integrity and innovation.

The Acumen Fellows Program: Run by Acumen, a global non-profit venture fund, this program selects leaders from around the world who are tackling poverty and social injustice. The fellowship includes leadership development, mentorship, and a network that fosters ethical decision-making and sustainable impact.

The Obama Foundation Leaders: Africa Program: This initiative identifies and supports emerging leaders across Africa who are working on community-driven solutions for social change. Through training, mentorship, and networking, the program aims to cultivate ethical leadership and inspire collective action for positive societal impact.

These programs exemplify how investing in ethical leadership development can empower individuals to lead with integrity, accountability, and a commitment to social justice, thereby fostering positive change in their communities and beyond.

Grassroots Advocacy and Community Organizing

Grassroots advocacy and community organizing empower individuals and communities to mobilize collective action, advocate for policy change, and hold decision-makers accountable.

The Black Lives Matter Global Network, founded in 2013 following the acquittal of George Zimmerman in the killing of Trayvon Martin, has emerged as a powerful grassroots movement advocating for racial justice and police reform. Through protests, advocacy campaigns, and community organizing efforts, Black Lives Matter activists have challenged systemic racism, elevated the voices of marginalized communities, and mobilized support for policy changes at local, national, and international levels.

Challenging the neutrality paradigm requires a commitment to justice, equity, and accountability in decision-making processes. By embracing alternative approaches that prioritize justice, equity, and accountability, individuals and institutions can challenge the neutrality paradigm and advance social justice agendas. Through intersectional justice, decolonizing approaches, and participatory democracy, we can create more inclusive and equitable decision-making processes that centre the voices and experiences of marginalized communities. By promoting media literacy, ethical leadership development, and grassroots advocacy, we can empower individuals to critically engage with complex issues and advocate for positive change in their communities and beyond.

By challenging the idea of neutrality and embracing justice, equity, and accountability, we can build a more inclusive and fair society. So, let's get out there and make a difference—our future depends on it!

In the end, the true measure of a society's progress lies not only in its grand achievements but also in its collective response to injustice and suffering. When neutrality morphs into indifference, it corrodes the very fabric of our communities, leaving behind a trail of missed opportunities for positive change. As we confront the harsh realities of our world, let us not succumb to the allure of neutrality, but rather embrace our inherent capacity for empathy and compassion. Each act of kindness, each moment of solidarity, and each voice raised against injustice contributes to the gradual transformation of our society. By rejecting apathy and fostering a culture of active engagement and social responsibility, we can pave the way for a brighter and more inclusive future where every individual is valued, heard, and empowered to thrive.

Future Perspectives and Approaches

Envisioning the evolving landscape of neutrality and fostering critical awareness in an increasingly complex world

23

The Future of Neutrality

"Neutrality is a negative word. It does not express what America ought to feel. We are not trying to keep out of trouble; we are trying to preserve the foundations on which peace may be rebuilt"

- Woodrow Wilson

As we navigate an era defined by rapid globalization, technological advancement, and evolving social dynamics, the concept of neutrality faces new challenges and opportunities. This discourse speculates on the evolving role of neutrality and its implications for the future of democracy, human rights, and social cohesion. By examining emerging trends and shifting power dynamics, let's explore how neutrality may adapt to meet the demands of an interconnected world.

The Changing Face of Neutrality

Navigating Technological Waters

In an increasingly digital world, the concept of technological neutrality takes centre stage. As technological innovations shape our interactions, economies, and societies, questions arise about the neutrality of algorithms, artificial intelligence, and digital platforms.

The debate over algorithmic bias and discrimination highlights the importance of ensuring technological neutrality in our decision-making processes. As algorithms increasingly influence everything from hiring decisions to criminal justice outcomes, we have concerns about the potential for bias and inequality perpetuated by opaque algorithms.

Information in the Age of Disinformation

The proliferation of information and the rise of disinformation challenge the neutrality of information ecosystems. As misinformation spreads rapidly through online platforms and social media, questions arise about the role of information intermediaries in preserving our neutrality and fostering informed public discourse.

The spread of misinformation and conspiracy theories during public health crises, such as the COVID-19 pandemic, underscores the need for platforms to prioritize information neutrality and combat the spread of false narratives. Platforms' decisions about content moderation and fact-checking mechanisms have significant implications for the neutrality of online information ecosystems.

Ethics in Technology

As technological advancements continue to reshape our society, the future of neutrality must grapple with ethical considerations in technology development and deployment. Questions arise about the neutrality of technologies such as facial recognition, surveillance systems, and autonomous weapons, which have the potential to impact human rights and civil liberties.

The development of facial recognition technology raises concerns about privacy, surveillance, and bias. As governments and private companies deploy facial recognition systems for law enforcement, border control, and surveillance purposes, questions arise about the neutrality of these technologies and their potential for discriminatory outcomes, particularly against marginalized communities.

Transparency and Accountability in Algorithms

Ensuring algorithmic transparency and accountability is essential for preserving neutrality in decision-making processes. As algorithms increasingly influence various aspects of our lives, from healthcare to finance, questions arise about the neutrality of algorithmic decision-making and the potential for unintended consequences.

The use of predictive algorithms in criminal justice systems raises questions about fairness and bias. As these algorithms are used to assess risk and make decisions about bail, sentencing, and parole, concerns arise about the neutrality of these systems and their potential for perpetuating racial disparities in the criminal justice system.

Implications for Democracy, Human Rights, and Social Harmony

Democracy and Informed Engagement

The future of neutrality has profound implications for the health of democratic institutions and processes. As political polarization intensifies and misinformation proliferates, questions arise about the role of neutrality in fostering informed civic engagement and preserving democratic norms.

The erosion of trust in democratic institutions and the rise of populist movements challenge traditional notions of political neutrality. As citizens increasingly question the neutrality of media, government institutions, and electoral processes, the future of democracy hinges on restoring public trust and promoting inclusive, transparent governance.

Human Rights and Social Justice

Neutrality plays a crucial role in upholding human rights and promoting social justice. As global challenges such as climate change, refugee crises, and systemic inequality intensify, questions arise about the neutrality of international institutions and the effectiveness of collective action in addressing these challenges.

The United Nations' Universal Declaration of Human Rights embodies the principle of neutrality in promoting fundamental human rights and freedoms. However, questions arise about the neutrality of international interventions in conflicts and humanitarian crises, particularly when geopolitical interests and power dynamics come into play.

Unity and Inclusion

The future of neutrality also impacts social cohesion and inclusion in diverse societies. As societies grapple with issues of identity, belonging, and cultural diversity, questions arise about the neutrality of public discourse and the role of institutions in fostering inclusive communities.

The rise of identity-based politics and ethnonationalism challenges traditional notions of neutrality in public discourse. As debates over immigration, multiculturalism, and social welfare policies intensify, the future of social cohesion hinges on promoting dialogue, understanding, and respect for diverse perspectives.

Reimagining Democratic Institutions

The future of neutrality in democracy requires reimagining traditional democratic institutions to better reflect the diverse needs and perspectives of modern societies. Embracing participatory democracy, deliberative processes, and inclusive decision-making mechanisms can foster greater citizen engagement and trust in democratic processes.

Participatory budgeting initiatives, such as those implemented in cities like Paris and Chicago, empower residents to directly participate in allocating public funds and shaping local priorities. By decentralizing decision-making power and amplifying marginalized voices, participatory democracy challenges traditional top-down governance structures and fosters greater accountability and transparency.

Strengthening Human Rights Protections

Upholding human rights in the future requires strengthening international mechanisms for accountability and promoting a culture of human rights at all levels of society. Embracing a human rights-based approach to policymaking and governance can help address systemic inequalities and promote social justice.

The establishment of international human rights treaties and mechanisms, such as the International Criminal Court (ICC) and the United Nations Human Rights Council (UNHRC), underscores the importance of global cooperation in advancing human rights. By holding states accountable for human rights violations and promoting dialogue and cooperation, these institutions contribute to the future of neutrality in upholding human rights.

Fostering Inclusive Communities

Promoting social cohesion and inclusion in diverse societies requires addressing structural barriers and fostering a sense of belonging for all members of society. Embracing cultural diversity, promoting intercultural dialogue, and investing in social cohesion initiatives can help bridge divides and build resilient communities.

The integration of refugees and migrants into host communities presents opportunities to foster social cohesion and solidarity. By providing access to education, employment, and social services, countries can promote the inclusion and integration of refugees and migrants, contributing to the future of neutrality in fostering inclusive societies.

The future of neutrality in an interconnected world is shaped by technological advancements, social dynamics, and geopolitical shifts. By grappling with ethical considerations in technology development, reimagining democratic institutions, strengthening human rights protections, and fostering inclusive communities, we can navigate the complexities of the future and shape a world that prioritizes justice, equity, and human dignity for all.

As our world hurtles forward, shaped by tech, society, and geopolitics, the evolution of neutrality holds immense importance. By grappling with ethical tech development, rethinking democratic processes, and fostering inclusivity, we can steer towards a future that champions justice, equality, and human dignity for all.

24

Embracing critical awareness on Neutrality in a complex world

"Neutrality, like fidelity, is a relational term. One does not declare oneself neutral; one becomes neutral in the eyes of others"

- Elise Boulding

As we conclude our exploration into the complexities of neutrality and its ramifications for our society, the resounding echoes of Martin Niemöller's mournful words linger in our consciousness.

First, they came for the socialists, and I did not speak out—because I was not a socialist.

Then they came for the trade unionists, and I did not speak out—because I was not a trade unionist.

Then they came for the Jews, and I did not speak out—because I was not a Jew.

Then they came for me—and there was no one left to speak for me.

—Martin Niemöller

The poignant words of Martin Niemöller's renowned poem, "First They Came," reverberate through history, serving as a solemn reminder of the dangers of remaining silent in the face of injustice. Niemöller, a prominent Protestant pastor in Germany, boldly opposed Adolf Hitler's regime and endured seven years of imprisonment in concentration camps as a consequence of his defiance.

The poem unfolds like a chilling narrative, each stanza bearing witness to the gradual erosion of societal values and the perilous consequences of apathy. "First they came for the socialists," he writes, highlighting the initial targets of oppression. Yet, in his retelling, he confesses his silence, acknowledging that he did not speak out because he did not identify as a socialist.

The poem's progression intensifies as he recounts subsequent waves of persecution. "Then they came for the trade unionists," he laments, underscoring the systematic dismantling of organized labour and the suppression of dissenting voices. Again, he admits to his silence, rationalizing his inaction by distancing himself from the targeted group.

With each verse, the poem unveils the insidious nature of tyranny, as he chronicles the descent into darkness. "Then they came for the Jews," he writes, capturing the horrors of the Holocaust and the genocide perpetrated against millions. Despite the atrocities unfolding around him, his confession remains unchanged—he did not speak out, for he was not among the persecuted.

The poem's haunting conclusion serves as a sobering revelation. "Then they came for me," he declares, confronting the chilling reality that indifference breeds impunity. In the absence of solidarity and collective action, there is no refuge from oppression. As the poet stands alone, abandoned by those who failed to raise their voices, the profound implications of complacency resonate deeply.

Here, let me recall the words of Holocaust survivor Abe Foxman: "The crematoria, gas chambers in Auschwitz and elsewhere did not begin with bricks, it began with words...evil words, hateful words, antisemitic words, words of prejudice. And they were permitted to proceed to violence because of the absence of words which implies the neutral mindset of people." His poignant reflection underscores the insidious nature of neutrality, highlighting its role in enabling atrocities through silence and inaction.

His verse transcends its historical context, serving as a cautionary tale for generations to come. It warns against the seductive allure of neutrality and the perilous consequences of moral indifference. In a world besieged by injustice and tyranny, the echoes of Niemöller and Abe

Foxman's words compel us to stand vigilant, to speak out against oppression wherever it may arise, lest we too find ourselves bereft of allies when the oppressor comes for us.

As you reach the conclusion of this exploration into the nuances of neutrality and its impact on our society, I urge you to reflect deeply on the ideas presented and consider the implications for our collective future. Throughout this journey, we have examined the concept of neutrality from various angles, uncovering both its potential benefits and its inherent limitations. Now, as we prepare to move forward, it is essential to arm ourselves with critical awareness and vigilance against the pitfalls of neutral thinking.

From now on, let's reject the passive acceptance of neutral narratives that uphold the status quo. Instead, let's embrace a stance of active engagement and critical inquiry, amplifying marginalized voices and challenging entrenched systems of oppression. As you navigate the complexities of our society, resist the temptation to passively accept neutral narratives that uphold backwardness and hinder progress. Embrace a stance of critical engagement and active inquiry, challenging assumptions, questioning authority, and seeking out diverse perspectives. By doing so, you can help dismantle the barriers that stand in the way of positive social change and contribute to the advancement of a more just and equitable world.

Furthermore, understanding issues correctly requires more than just neutrality; it demands empathy, compassion, and a commitment to social justice. As you engage with complex issues, strive to listen deeply to the voices of those most affected, amplifying marginalized perspectives and centring the experiences of those whose voices are often silenced.

In closing, remain vigilant against the allure of neutrality and embrace the responsibility of actively shaping the future of our society. Reject complacency and apathy, and champion critical awareness and ethical action. Together, we can build a world that reflects our highest ideals of justice, equality, and human dignity.

Thank you for embarking on this journey with me. May your path be illuminated by the light of knowledge, empathy, courage, and unwavering resolve.

With Best Wishes
Author